William J Fay 2.25
#1849

MARK'S STORY OF JESUS

MARK'S STORY OF JESUS

Werner H. Kelber

FORTRESS PRESS   PHILADELPHIA

Library of Congress Cataloging in Publication Data

Kelber, Werner H
   Mark's story of Jesus.

   A revision of the author's series of lectures
delivered at the Episcopal Lay Academy in Houston, Tex.,
during Lent 1978.
   1. Jesus Christ—History of doctrines—Early church,
ca. 30-600—Addresses, essays, lectures. 2. Bible.
N.T. Mark—Criticism, interpretation, etc.—Addresses,
essays, lectures. I. Title.
BT198.K44   232.9'01   78-14668
ISBN 0-8006-1355-4

7414K78   Printed in the United States of America   1-1355

To
my parents
my parents-in-law
and Magda Kelber

Contents

Preface

The primary objective of this book is an interpretative retelling of Mark's story of the life and death of Jesus. Mark's Gospel is viewed as a dramatically plotted journey of Jesus. Throughout the Gospel Jesus is depicted as being in movement from one place to another. He journeys through Galilee, undertakes six boat trips on and across the Lake of Galilee, travels from Galilee to Jerusalem, makes three trips into the temple, and toward the end signals the return to Galilee. Mark invites the reader to follow Jesus on this journey which leads through a series of unexpected experiences and crises. But the reader who follows Jesus' journey to the end will be shown a way out of the crisis.

This book has grown out of a series of lectures delivered at the Episcopal Lay Academy in Houston, Texas, during Lent 1978. The lectures were presented before a general audience and hence intended to be nontechnical both in style and content. This book, although a considerable revision of the lectures, likewise addresses a readership of nonspecialists. Footnotes, technical language, and scholarly discussions have been deliberately avoided.

By and large this interpretation of Mark follows the Second Edition of the Revised Standard Version New Testament Text of 1971. At a number of points, however, recent scholarly developments demand corrections. Whenever this is the case, the reader is offered the RSV translation and alerted to the new version.

It is a pleasure to acknowledge the hospitality shown to me by the organizers and members of the Episcopal Lay Academy. Their critical questions were a constant source of stimulation for me. In addition I should like to thank four persons who have notably contributed to the making of this book: Mrs. Josephine Monaghan, an extremely competent typist; Kevin B. Maxwell, S.J., and David W. Rutledge, both Ph.D. candidates at the Department of Religious Studies, Rice University; and my wife, Mary Ann.

WERNER H. KELBER

Introduction

Both in study and in worship the Gospel of Mark has generally been treated as a collection of short stories. Articles and monographs single out specific aspects of the Gospel, commentaries are prone to break up the narrative flow, and translations are deeply influenced by this piecemeal approach. Reading only sections of Mark in worship likewise fractures our vision, perpetuating habits of hearing and reading which are detrimental to a total comprehension. Because we have focused on the individual stories *in* Mark we have not really come to know the story *of* Mark. This book is designed to introduce the reader to a single coherent story, Mark's story of Jesus' life and death. From a literary perspective the reader is therefore advised to approach the Markan story as he or she would any other story: to read the whole story from beginning to end, to observe the characters and the interplay among them, to watch for the author's clues regarding the plot, to discern the plot development, to identify scenes of crisis and recognition, and to view the story's resolution in the light of its antecedent logic.

In reading Mark one must refrain from injecting Matthean, Lukan, or Johannine elements into his Gospel. Mark deserves to be read on his own terms. This is all the more important since it has become evident that our four evangelists have given us four rather different stories of the life and death of Jesus. Among other things, it was this recognition of their differences which led to the acceptance of four Gospels into the New Testament. Indeed, if the four Gospels were identical, the choice of just one would have been entirely sufficient. The explanation for these four different gospel stories is to be found in the diverse circumstances surrounding their compositions. Each Gospel was written by a different

author, at a different time in history, and for a different readership. Each Gospel is shaped by specific cultural attachments,
characteristic literary conventions, and distinct sociopolitical and
religious conditions. To read Mark through the glasses of the other
Gospels would violate the integrity of Mark and misapprehend the
nature of all four gospel writers. Therefore if we wish to grasp
Mark's story, we must in a sense lose sight of Matthew's, Luke's,
and John's stories. The reading of Mark demands a single-minded
concentration on the Markan text.

The discovery of four separate gospel identities raises the issue
of the Gospels' historical reliability. In plain terms, if the Gospels
give us four different Jesus stories, which one is historically accu-
rate? Granted that our evangelists address different people at different times and circumstances, are they not obliged to give us the
facts about Jesus? This is a difficult question, and one that has
been debated over the past two hundred years in Christian theology
and biblical studies. Perhaps the most important contribution biblical studies have made in this century to our understanding of the
Gospels was to turn the balance in the struggle over the nature of
the Gospels—historical versus religious—decisively in favor of the
latter. The evangelists are now recognized as religious writers, not
as historians, and their Gospels are appreciated as religious documents, not as historiographies.

Precisely what does it mean to be a religious writer in contrast
to being a historian? Negatively, the prime motivation for our
evangelists to write a gospel was not to reproduce the exact facts
concerning the historical Jesus of approximately A.D. 30. The
evangelists are not historians or professors of history who recon-
struct the past for the purpose of advancing factual knowledge.
Positively, the prime motivation for our evangelists to write a gospel has been to make the Jesus of A.D. 30 relevant to their own
(the evangelists') time. Their deepest concern, not unlike that of
theologians, priests, and ministers, is to reinterpret the Jesus of
the past for the present. Reinterpretation, however, does not mean
exact reproduction. Reinterpretation entails a process of creative
rewriting and in part even reconceptualizing. This process is demanded by changing times and changing cultural conditions. Un-

less Jesus is reinterpreted he ceases to be a live option. In this spirit each evangelist reactivates the message and memory of Jesus in a manner both meaningful and intelligible to his readers.

If we conceive of the Gospel of Mark as a reinterpretation of the life and death of Jesus, who then is Mark, the author, and under what historical circumstances does he write his Gospel? The Gospel was originally written anonymously. Later ecclesiastical tradition suggested a number of authorial identifications, but biblical scholarship has by and large not accepted these suggestions. To this day Mark has remained an anonymous Jewish Christian author. When throughout this book we refer to the author as Mark, we do so as a matter of convenience, without thereby intending to make a historical identification.

We are somewhat better informed about the historical circumstances surrounding the Gospel's composition. A scholarly consensus is beginning to emerge which points to Galilee, or southern Syria, as a likely place for the Markan Gospel. The Gospel's internal logic more than external evidence suggests such an area. We shall observe that this Gospel appears to have been written from a northern, Galilean-Syrian viewpoint and over against a distinct southern viewpoint. As for the time of the writing, an increasing number of scholars assume a date after the Roman-Jewish War (A.D. 66–74). Again, the Gospel's internal evidence favors this time in history. Some of the events of this war seem to be reflected in chapter 13 of the Gospel. Moreover we shall see that the author exhibits an unusual preoccupation with the Jerusalem temple and its destruction, an event which occurred at the peak of the war in A.D. 70. The Gospel's total logic, finally, would also seem to support a composition in the aftermath of the Roman-Jewish War.

If the crucifixion of Jesus is dated approximately A.D. 30, then the Markan Gospel was not written until more than forty years thereafter. Those forty years were a time of the greatest violence and bloodshed in Israel's history, culminating in the Roman victory over the Jewish nation. As Roman acts of oppression increased, Jewish reactions intensified. Sporadic uprising among the Jews led to open rebellion, which in turn evolved into organized war efforts. To all intents and purposes Roman victory was assured by the capture of Jerusalem in A.D. 70. The city was destroyed, the temple burnt to the ground, and Israel ceased to exist as a political nation until the establishment of the state of Israel in 1948.

The early Christians will not have remained unaffected by this catastrophe. The majority of the early Christians were Jews, and their allegiance to Jesus did not for the most part diminish their loyalty to the Jerusalem temple. To the extent that it is historically prudent to differentiate between Jews and Jewish Christians at this early stage, Jerusalem and its temple will have been the focal point for virtually all of them. The Roman superpower will hardly have been capable of making the subtle distinction between Jews and Jewish Christians. For these reasons the destruction of the center will have been a traumatic experience for Jews as well as Christians.

The Roman-Jewish War and the destruction of the temple provide the broad historical backdrop for the Gospel of Mark, and the reader may keep these events in mind in reading the Gospel. There may be a connection between the loss of the national center and Mark's writing the story of Jesus. In any case the story he tells appears to be both meaningful and intelligible when read against the background of Israel's searing tragedy.

1

The Mystery
of the
Kingdom

MARK 1:1—4:34

In the first part of his gospel composition Mark introduces Jesus as a man of authority who travels throughout Galilee, preaching and promoting the Kingdom of God through extraordinary deeds of power. The nature of the Kingdom is such that it provokes antagonism, dividing the audience into insiders who can perceive and outsiders who cannot.

PREPARING THE WAY

The titular inscription "The Gospel According to Mark" which the reader will find placed over the text is not generally regarded as part of the original gospel text. In the absence of this inscription the opening words 1:1 deserve our special attention. Set apart from 1:2 they function as the proper title to the gospel: "The beginning of the gospel about Jesus Christ, the Son of God." This title, as all titles, discloses what in the mind of the author is the nature and purpose of his work. By making "gospel" the subject of this title, Mark designates his whole composition as gospel. This is not to be taken for granted, because neither Matthew nor Luke nor John chose to call their literary productions a gospel. In early

Christian terminology *gospel* commonly denotes a message or an
announcement, a proclamation delivered in oral form. Prophets
and apostles preach the gospel news traveling from one place to
another. Paul the apostle knows gospel primarily in its orally delivered form (1 Cor. 9:18; 15:1; 2 Cor. 2:12; Gal. 2:2; Rom. 10:16–
17), and Mark himself is familiar with Jesus the preacher of the
gospel (1:14) and the followers' preaching of the gospel to all the
nations (13:10). What is remarkable therefore about the use of
"gospel" in Mark 1:1 is its titular designation of a written story.
As far as is known, this is the first time in early Christian literature that a story about Jesus' life and death is written down under
the title "gospel." Not words of Jesus but a biographical narrative
about the life and death of Jesus constitutes the Markan Gospel.

In view of the traditional oral nature of gospel, Mark's concept
must be considered a significant departure from early Christian
usage of gospel. By writing a story and calling it gospel Mark in-
spires people to read his gospel story. This new concept of reading
a gospel makes heavy demands on Markan readers, for what Mark
communicates, the gospel message, is not easily or directly grasped
by the reader. The meaning of Mark's gospel is not encapsulated
in a spoken message affecting the audience at the moment of hearing. The essence of his gospel is not even apprehended in a single,
pivotal saying such as 1:15, which features the central message
preached by the Markan Jesus. There is only one way to understand Mark's gospel message, and that is to read his whole story
from 1:1 to 16:8.

Moreover Mark refers in his title to "the beginning of the gospel." He regards his total written story as the beginning of the
gospel. The Markan text prepares the reader for the appropriation
of the gospel message. It is only after the gospel story has been
read from start to finish that the reader knows Mark's gospel
message and can adopt it for his or her life situation. In this sense,
reading the Gospel of Mark is but the beginning of the gospel's
actualization in real life.

The principal character in Mark's gospel story is Jesus, presented in the titular verse as "Christ, the Son of God." Before
Jesus himself speaks in the gospel story and before he is desig-

nated by the heavenly voice, Mark has introduced him to the reader as a figure of extraordinary authority. The precise nature of his authority, that is, the meaning of *Christ* and *Son of God*, is not disclosed by the title, and the reader should avoid injecting non-Markan preconceptions. Mark, the writer of the gospel story, does not convey the complete identity of Jesus in a single verse, not even in the titular verse. The full understanding of this Jesus of authority hinges on the reading of Mark's entire story about him.

Following the title verse Mark cites an Old Testament quotation which announces the appearance of a messenger figure (1:2-3). The chief function of this messenger is communicated to the reader by the method of reiteration. Twice, in verses 1:2 and 1:3, the quotation characterizes him as a preparer of the way. Since the messenger is identified in 1:4 as John the Baptist, it can be assumed that John is to prepare the way of Jesus, the Gospel's principal character. The very first time Mark alludes to an aspect of Jesus' life, he does so in terms of a "way." The reader knows that Jesus will be traveling a way. We shall observe that the Markan Jesus is indeed in constant movement from place to place, from region to region, frequently back and forth, and all the way from life to death. Jesus' whole career is conceived in Mark as a journey. The reader will understand Jesus, his life and his death, by paying close attention to the points of departure and arrival, to the directions and goals of his travels. There is a logic to Jesus' journey, and to grasp that logic is to grasp the meaning of his mission and identity.

In many ways John the Baptist is a model for Jesus. John is active in the wilderness (1:4,6), and Jesus will go into the wilderness (1:12). John is a preacher (1:4,7), and so is Jesus (1:14-15). John demands repentance from his audience (1:4), and Jesus likewise demands repentance (1:15). John forgives sins (1:4-5), and so will Jesus (2:5,10). Most importantly in Mark, both John and Jesus will die a violent death (6:14-29; 15:21-39). Yet the differences between John and Jesus are still more obvious. John is an ascetic, solitary personality (1:6), and his disciples are instructed to practice fasting (2:18). Jesus enters into table fellowship with tax collectors and sinners (2:15-17), and his disciples

are not instructed to observe the rules of fasting (2:18) and washing hands before meals (7:2). Furthermore John is not depicted as
a traveling preacher as Jesus is. John is stationed in the Jordan
Valley, presumably near the Dead Sea, because his ministry at-
tracts "all the country of Judea, and all the people of Jerusalem"
(1:5). Since Judea and Jerusalem are the heartland of the Jewish
population, John's influence extends primarily to Jewish people.
John is the messenger who is prophesied in Jewish Scripture (1:2),
anticipated in the Jewish world (6:15; 8:28), and thus he ministers
to the Jewish people. Jesus, who according to the forerunner's
own words is mightier than John (1:7–8), will not be stationed
at a single place nor will his ministry be focused on Judea and
Jerusalem. We shall see that Jesus' early travels are designed to
cover Galilee, an area to the north of Judea and Jerusalem, and
to include the Jewish as well as the Gentile part of the population.
Working in a manner different from John's, ministering in an area
set apart from John's, Jesus' mission and message will likewise
be different from that of John's.

According to 1:9, Jesus is the man who "came from Nazareth
of Galilee." From the outset Jesus is "coming," in motion from
place to place. Since apart from the title this is the moment Jesus
is introduced into the story, the identifications of Nazareth and
Galilee must be considered significant. Mark does not give us an
account of Jesus' birth and never mentions Bethlehem in his Gospel. The reader of Mark's Gospel must take this to heart. Whatever the place and the circumstances of Jesus' birth, as far as
Mark is concerned Jesus is the man from Nazareth in Galilee, and
it is from there that he undertakes his first journey to John the
Baptist.

One succinct sentence reports the baptism of Jesus by John
(1:9). The emphasis is on what is not ordinarily part of John's
water baptizing: the opening of the heavens, the descent of the
Spirit, and the heavenly voice (1:10–11). These latter events
distinguish the baptism of this Galilean from that of all the Ju-
deans. When Jesus emerges from the water he sees "the heavens
opened and the Spirit descending" (1:10). Neither crowds nor
John observe these extraordinary occurrences. Jesus' reception of

the Spirit is an act of the greatest privacy, inaccessible to outside witnesses. Among the characters in the Gospel's story, nobody knows of the descent of the Spirit at this point. The reader alone has been made the privileged witness! The heavenly voice, addressed to Jesus personally, identifies him as God's beloved Son (1:11). Spoken in conjunction with the bestowal of the Spirit, the designation Son of God has now received a specific content. That Jesus is the Son of God means that he has been singled out, from all those coming to John, by the reception of the power of God's Spirit.

The Spirit, henceforth the driving force in the life of Jesus, "immediately" propels him into the wilderness. The subsequent temptation by Satan (1:12–13) gives a major clue to Jesus' ministry. Endowed with the Spirit, he is driven into a confrontation with Satan, because the defeat of the powers of evil is, negatively, the principal objective of his mission. In whatever form and person Satan appears, Jesus will be in opposition to him. The reference to wild beasts and angels alludes to his triumph over the Satanic temptation. By living in fellowship with wild beasts while angels serve him, Jesus anticipates the realm of God. That is, positively, the purpose of his life: to bring the Kingdom of God.

There is a tight logic which controls the Markan story of 1:2–12 and sets the stage for the pivotal verses 1:14–15. The Baptist prepares the way which Jesus is to travel. Jesus enters upon the way by traveling to the Baptist. Equipped with the Spirit, he is driven into the wilderness to an initial encounter with Satan. Emerging victorious from that confrontation, he is now fully qualified to make his gospel announcement. To this end Jesus the Galilean returns to Galilee after John's imprisonment. Empowered with the Spirit and tested by Satan, he makes his first public announcement, which is solemnly qualified as "the gospel of God": "The right time has been fulfilled, and the Kingdom of God has arrived. [The RSV rendering with "is at hand" does not properly convey the Markan meaning.] Repent and believe in the gospel" (1:14–15). This pivotal message of the Kingdom's arrival announces the life program of the Markan Jesus. He is the proclaimer and bringer of the Kingdom; all aspects of his life and death are related to this mission of the Kingdom. Mark's gospel is in a special sense the gospel of the Kingdom; all aspects of his story must be viewed in light of Jesus' inaugural Kingdom proclamation. What exactly the nature of the Kingdom is the reader does not know at this point. But Mark has written the story of the Kingdom's arrival, and reading the complete story will disclose the contours of the Kingdom.

ARRIVAL OF THE KINGDOM

The calling of the four fishermen (1:16–20) accords a communal dimension to the Kingdom. While in the Gospel of John the Kingdom is defined as an entity not of this world (John 18:36), in Mark the Kingdom is entirely of this world. The news of the Kingdom's arrival is announced to people, and people are called into the service of the Kingdom. The Kingdom is the people of God. Simon and Andrew, James and John form its nucleus, and by following Jesus on his way they are privileged to learn the lesson regarding the Kingdom. At the end of the journey they will themselves be ready to function as "fishers of men" (1:17) on behalf of the Kingdom community. As the way of Jesus becomes that of the disciples the reader is likewise invited to participate in their pilgrimage. Traveling the way of Jesus the reader will find the key to Jesus' identity and the entrance to the Kingdom of God.

Leaving their place at the Lake of Galilee the four join Jesus on his way to the lakeside town of Capernaum. It is there that he will perform his first exorcism, that is, the casting out of an evil spirit (1:21–27). "Immediately" on a sabbath Jesus enters the synagogue and teaches with an authority unlike that of the scribes, the representatives of the Jerusalem establishment (cf. 3:22). Such is his authoritative teaching that an unclean spirit recognizes him as "Jesus of Nazareth" and "the Holy One of God" (1:24). The evil spirit makes the kind of identification which no human being, with one exception, will make in Mark's gospel story. There exists a bond of mutual recognition between the demonic spirits and the Spirit-filled Son of God. "Have you come to destroy

us?" (1:24), asks the unclean spirit. He realizes that Jesus' mission
is intended to oppose not merely a single exponent of evil but the
demonic power structure itself. After Jesus' initial confrontation
with Satan in the wilderness, this is now the first case of a power
struggle with the forces of Satan. The evil spirit, recognizing
Jesus and his authority, implores him not to overturn the demonic
realm of power, but Jesus rebukes him, and the result is the
convulsion and crushing defeat of the evil spirit.

"Immediately" afterwards Jesus enters the house of Simon
and heals his mother-in-law, who had been confined to bed with
a fever (1:29–31). That same evening those sick and possessed
with evil spirits in Capernaum are brought to the house, and
Jesus heals many of them. Yet strangely enough Jesus will not
permit the forces of evil to divulge his identity, "because they
knew him" (1:34; cf. 3:11–12). The only ones who recognize
Jesus are not to make him known! The reason the identity of the
Son of God must not be revealed at this point is that Jesus has
not yet lived his destined life to the end. It is only after he has
ended on the cross that he will have fulfilled his identity. Then
and only then can the Roman centurion make the one and only
appropriate confession (15:39). Once again we remember that
one has to travel the way to the end or read the story of Jesus'
journey to the closing line before a full understanding of Jesus,
the Son of God, can be reached.

We have observed Jesus on his first day in Capernaum healing many people stricken with diseases. This healing mission
constitutes an essential part of his message of the arrival of the
Kingdom. Since in the ancient world all physical and mental dis-
orders are assumed to have been caused by evil powers, Jesus'
healings amount to a frontal attack on the power structure of
evil. His confrontation with Satan in the wilderness has indeed
given a clue to the purpose of his life. He came to announce the
Kingdom of God and to initiate its arrival in opposition to the
forces which threaten and destroy human life. It is also noteworthy that the two examples Mark singles out from among the
many healings in Capernaum, the possessed man in the synagogue and Simon's mother-in-law, concern a suffering male and

a suffering female. This, we shall see, is not incidental to the logic of the Markan Kingdom story. The Kingdom is the people of God liberated from the forces of evil—males and females alike.

THE GALILEAN JOURNEY

The following morning Jesus goes to a lonely place to pray (1:35–38). Simon and the other disciples notice his absence in Capernaum, and they are reported to have "pursued him" (1:36). The point is not that Simon and those with him "follow" Jesus as loyal disciples but rather that they seek after him, disturbing his moment of peace and prayer. What they have planned is Jesus' return to Capernaum, the site of his earlier triumphs: "Everyone is looking for you" (1:37). What Jesus has in mind, however, is to move elsewhere (1:38). This is a first and very subtle indication of a disagreement between Jesus and his disciples. The disciples wish, understandably enough, to repeat the glory of the past day, while Jesus is oriented toward new places and the future. It is as if the disciples have an objective and goal in mind which may not exactly match the travel plans of Jesus. They will go along with Jesus, but it is not entirely clear whether they truly "follow" him on his way.

Having issued the call to move elsewhere, Jesus travels across the land of Galilee and to specific places in Galilee. At first glance this journey lacks a sense of logic and purposefulness, even to most commentators. Jesus travels through Galilee, back to Capernaum, along the Lake of Galilee, into a house, then to a synagogue, back again to the lakeside, and so forth. These travels give the appearance of aimless wanderings devoid of any clear sense of direction. They seem informal at best and erratic at worst. But this appearance of aimlessness, we shall see, is deceptive. We have normally focused our attention on the events occurring and the words spoken during the journey, and less on the journey itself. If we refocus our attention to the pattern of Jesus' journey, the purpose and effect of his Galilean mission will become evident. There are three major aspects, or shifts in direction, to this journey. Briefly, the first phase commences at Capernaum and features a journey through all of Galilee. It describes the overwhelming response to Jesus' mission. The second phase again begins at Capernaum and entails subsequent trips to a house, a synagogue, through the grainfields, and so forth. It signifies the mounting opposition to Jesus' Kingdom message. The third phase, overlapping with the second one, marks three trips to a lakeside setting where crowds assemble in ever growing numbers. These journeys to the lakeside gatherings anticipate the blueprint of the new community and signal the new direction across the Lake of Galilee.

With these clues to guide us it will now be profitable to retrace Jesus' route in greater detail. His authoritative exorcism and teaching in the synagogue of Capernaum was so out of the ordinary that his fame rapidly spread across the land of Galilee (1:28). After the healing of Simon's mother-in-law, "all" the sick of Capernaum are brought to him (1:32) and "the whole town" assembles in front of the house (1:33). The following morning Jesus seeks a lonely place (1:35) away from the crowds. From there, after ignoring the disciples' efforts to return to Capernaum, he sets out on his journey "throughout all Galilee" to preach and heal in the synagogues (1:39). Since his fame has already preceded him across Galilee (1:28), his personal appearance creates such a stir that he can "no longer openly enter a town" (1:45). Contrary to his original plans to enter towns (1:39), he now has to avoid towns and stay at "lonely places" (1:45; the RSV translation with "in the country" is imprecise). Unable to travel openly, bypassing towns yet still pursued by crowds, he returns to Capernaum (2:1), the place of his departure. But this time he goes to a private home, possibly that of Simon's mother-in-law, and not to the synagogue, the site which had founded his fame. His desire to shun the townspeople of Capernaum is evident. Yet word gets around, and the house is mobbed so that the paralytic has to be brought in through the roof (2:2–4).

Thus Mark gives us a vivid picture of Jesus' Galilean journey between his first and second visit to Capernaum. It touches off a response of growing proportions, starting in Capernaum, sweeping across Galilee, and affecting people from everywhere.

Jesus himself seems overwhelmed and almost incapacitated by
the masses. Although he will henceforth avoid towns, he will not
be able to escape the crowds. But he has to move on, because
his journey has only barely got under way.

During the second visit at Capernaum the journey takes on a
new dimension. Whereas until now Jesus was sought after by
what appear to have been sympathetic crowds, he is now also
pursued by hostile people. In the synagogue of Capernaum
scribal authorities hurl the heavy charge of blasphemy against
him (2:5-7). It is this very charge which in the end, uttered by
the high priest himself, will seal Jesus' death sentence (14:64).
Henceforth the shadow of death is cast over the journey. Mobbed
by friendly crowds and accused of blasphemy by the legal authorities, Jesus departs from Capernaum, evading the towns of Galilee.
His journey now takes him to the lakeside, a private home, the
grainfields, an anonymous synagogue, and a mountain. But the
opposition is never far away, pursuing and challenging him all
along. In the house of Levi his table fellowship with tax collectors
and sinners incurs the condemnation of a group of Pharisees
(2:15-17). The disciples' laxity in observing the rules of fasting
is met with criticism (2:18-19). His own supreme authority over
the sabbath finally provokes the plot on his life (2:23-3:6).

It is of course Jesus' message and lifestyle which generate the
mounting antagonism among the authorities. As his journey continues it becomes ever more obvious that the Kingdom he announces and puts into practice is diametrically opposed to the
conventional piety and morality guarded by the authorities. The
forgiveness of sins, the primary concern for sinners, the nonob-
servance of the days of fasting, and the repeal of the sabbath law
combine to erect a counterstructure to the traditional ordering of
human life. The Kingdom of God entails a new lifestyle, a new
sense of priority, a new community. New wine is for fresh wine-
skins (2:22). The nature of the Kingdom is such that its King is
unacceptable to the Jerusalem authorities. A deep logic unites
the Kingdom of God and the death of the King. The Jesus who
breaks with his opponents by charging them with "hardness of
heart" (3:5) knows of his personal ending. Before his opponents

have entered into the conspiracy against his life (3:6), he has already anticipated his violent death (2:20). His journey is going to be a journey unto death.

We have observed Jesus' passage across Galilee in conjunction with the warm response of the masses, and his travels through rural areas accompanied by rising opposition. A third aspect of his journey concerns three trips to the lakeside. It was at the lakeside, we remember, that the first four disciples had been called into service as the nucleus of the Kingdom community. Jesus' first trip back to the lakeside occurs after the charge of blasphemy. Pressed by serious opposition as well as mounting enthusiasm, Jesus leaves Capernaum and returns to the lakeside setting. There he is met by "the whole crowd" (2:13). Unimpeded by opposition forces, he uses the opportunity for teaching and the calling of a fifth disciple (2:13–14). With the opposition in close pursuit after him, the lakeside functions as a place of refuge, of undisturbed teaching, and of the formation of a growing body of followers.

The second trip back to the lakeside follows in the wake of the first announcement of a death plot (3:6). Together with the disciples Jesus "withdraws" from the threat on his life to the lakeside setting (3:7). Upon arriving he encounters the largest crowd ever, a multitude of phenomenal proportions and regional diversity (3:8). Jesus' reputation has clearly passed beyond the borders of Galilee. The crowds have come not only from Galilee but also from Judea and Jerusalem, from Idumea and beyond the Jordan, from Tyre and Sidon. Judging from these diverse regions, the people are no longer limited to the Jewish nation. Galilee, Judea, Jerusalem, and possibly Idumea, to the south of Judea, are largely representative of Jewish people. But Tyre and Sidon, two towns on the Mediterranean coast to the north of Galilee, and the area across the Jordan river are primarily populated by Gentiles. The multitude which has gathered at the lakeside is therefore a mixed group consisting of Jews and Gentiles alike. As was the case at Jesus' first public performance in the synagogue of Capernaum (1:24), the unclean spirits recognize his identity as Son of God (3:11). But as Jesus had imposed silence upon the

spirits on that evening in Capernaum (1:34), he now also orders
them not to make him publicly known (3:12). What has occurred
at the lakeside is but a foreshadowing of things to come. Thus
far the ideal community is the result of spontaneous responses
to Jesus and his message. But Jesus has already ordered a boat
(3:9), initiating the new direction across the Lake of Galilee.
What we shall observe in the following chapter is Jesus using the
boat for the purpose of traveling himself into Gentile territory
and mapping out the geographical contours of this ecumenical,
Jewish-Gentile community, the Kingdom of God.

No sooner has the full ecumenical shape of the new community
come into view than Jesus proceeds to appoint its leadership. He
leaves the lakeside and goes up to a mountain. The mountain is
a place of great significance: it is the site of revelation. (On
Mount Sinai Moses encounters God and receives the divine com-
mandments.) In an act of momentous significance Jesus appoints twelve disciples as leaders over the new community, and
singles out three among them by special names (3:14–19). These
twelve, and especially the Three, will henceforth receive all the
instructions and information necessary to be able to function as
the leaders of the new community. That not all is well with this
leadership structure is impressed upon the reader by the shocking
final clause, "Judas Iscariot, who betrayed him" (3:19). This is
the first time the reader learns of the enemy within.

The first withdrawal to the lakeside, we recall, had followed
the charge of blasphemy, and the second trip was undertaken in
the wake of the death plot. The third and last trip is preceded by
a climactic confrontation between Jesus and opposition forces,
in which the charge of blasphemy resurfaces. After the appointment of the Twelve Jesus enters a house (the RSV rendering
with "he went home" is inaccurate) and is immediately hard
pressed by a crowd (3:19–20). Next his relatives are reported to
be on the way to seize Jesus because they consider him mentally
deranged (3:21). They want him removed from the public eye
because he has, in their judgment, made a spectacle of himself
and brought shame on the family. While the relatives are on the
way to the house, the scribal authorities from Jerusalem appear

again and reinforce the charge made by the family: Jesus is possessed by the devil (3:22). Jesus dissociates himself from the scribes and their accusation in the strongest terms possible (3:23–27) and returns their earlier charge of blasphemy. All sins are forgiven but the sin against the Holy Spirit, which is to mistake the works of the Son of God for those of Satan (3:28–30).

In the meantime "those close to him" have arrived at the house and are now clearly identified as Jesus' blood relatives (3:31). Jesus is in the house surrounded by a crowd, the insiders, while his family is outside, in the position of outsiders (3:32). After he is informed of his family's arrival, Jesus identifies those around him as the true family of God. In contrast to the insiders, he has left the family and scribes standing outside, thus reinforcing their status as outsiders. There is room in the Kingdom for all people except those who regard Jesus as the epitome of evil, be they the religious authorities or members of his own family.

THE KINGDOM SPEECH

Following his dramatic refutation of the powers of opposition, Jesus undertakes his third and last trip to the lakeside (4:1). Again it is the locale of friendly crowds and Jesus' teaching, but it will also serve as the place for a further definition of the followers of Jesus. Surrounded by "a very large crowd" Jesus enters the boat which he had ordered earlier (3:9) and moves out into the lake. His teaching from the boat, or as Mark puts it, "on the lake," indicates both the necessary distancing from the pressing crowds and the impending voyage across the lake. Of the "many things" Jesus teaches to the crowds "in parables" (4:2) Mark gives as a sample the parable of the sower (4:3–9).

Afterwards, in a notable change of scenery, Jesus is alone with the Twelve and "those who were about him" (4:10). This latter group appears to match the very people who had earlier "sat about him" in the house, the true family of God (3:34). It is to the Twelve and these closest followers that Jesus then utters the solemn statement, "To you has been given the mystery of the Kingdom of God" (4:11). With this extraordinary word the

Twelve and a group of followers have received a new and privileged status. The Twelve and "those about him" have the key to
the mystery of the Kingdom of God. They know as nobody else
knows. The Twelve and "those about him" have the inside
information. They are the insiders.

Important as the insider designation is, the reader is advised to
pay equal attention to Jesus' definition of outsiders. Outsiders,
the Markan Jesus continues, are people who see and yet do not
perceive, who hear and still do not understand (4:12). A surprising application of this outsider definition will at a later point
provide a dramatic turning point in the Markan story. For the
time being, a clear distinction is drawn between the Twelve and
"those about him" who are initiated into the mystery of the Kingdom, and the crowds, which as yet cannot receive the full message of the Kingdom.

Is it possible to say something at this point about the nature of
the mystery of the Kingdom of God? Jesus himself gives the
clues. In a climactic speech exclusively addressed to the insiders, he initiates them into the mystery of the Kingdom of God
(4:13–32). The world is unlike the Kingdom. People are suffering
and Satan is still powerful. Yet in the end there will be victory,
"thirtyfold and sixtyfold and a hundredfold" (4:14–20). If something is hidden, it is so only for the purpose of making a breakthrough toward light (4:21–23). The conduct at present deter-
mines one's outcome in the future (4:24–25). The seeds of the
Kingdom of God have been sown, and its process of growth is
inevitable (4:26–29). The minuteness of the Kingdom's em-
bryonic state provides a dramatic contrast to the magnitude of its
full growth (4:30–32). These are all clues to the mystery of the
Kingdom of God, and together they reveal the Kingdom in terms
of a process of growth. A beginning has been made and the Kingdom has arrived. But it will pass through a period of tribulation
and persecution. The Kingdom will enter an eclipse, but at some
future point it will emerge in global splendor, visible to all. In
short, the Kingdom entails a history and development—that is
its mystery. The seed has been sown, suffering and persecution
are part of the growth process, and full realization is yet to come.

That is what the Twelve and "those about him" must know as they join Jesus on his voyage across the lake.

SUMMARY

Mark narrates in 1:1—4:34 the story of John the Baptist preparing the way and of Jesus accomplishing the first part of this way. Authorized by the Spirit, Jesus introduces himself as the proclaimer of the Kingdom and specifies its arrival as the objective of his journey. His travelings across Galilee, through areas outside towns, and to the lakeside illuminate the nature of the Kingdom as well as positive and negative responses to it. The Kingdom is neither identifiable with a specific place in this world, be it a house, a town, a synagogue, or the fields, nor is it an otherworldly entity. The Kingdom of God is people, and it has arrived wherever people are liberated from the forces of evil. Although the ecumenical nature of the Kingdom is revealed in one instance, the Kingdom is still shrouded in mystery. The mystery surrounding the Kingdom of God is that it is still in progress and not an accomplished fact. The Kingdom is in the process of becoming. Hence Jesus must continue his journey toward the fulfillment of his objective. Nobody knows this mystery but the privileged insiders who will join him across the lake. Nobody, that is, but you, the reader. Mark has initiated his readers into the mystery of the Kingdom's ongoing history and made us privileged insiders who can partake in the voyages on and across the Lake of Galilee.

2

The Blindness
of the
Disciples

MARK 4:35—8:21

With the help of the boat prepared earlier (3:9; 4:1), Jesus and his disciples now undertake a series of trips on and across the Lake of Galilee. These boat trips combine into a purposeful itinerary which gives logic and unity to the section 4:35—8:21.

VOYAGE TO GENTILES AND JEWS

At the outset of the story traditionally called the stilling of the storm (4:35–41), the reader learns that the initiative for the crossing of the lake proceeds from Jesus (4:35). Whatever the meaning and significance of this first voyage, it and all subsequent voyages are willed and ordered by him. While Jesus and his disciples are traversing the lake, a storm arises, fills the boat with water, and threatens to drown the occupants. Overcome by panic the disciples arouse the sleeping Jesus: "Teacher, do you not care if we perish?" (Matthew and Luke will moderate Mark 4:38, the disciples' reproach of Jesus. Matt. 8:25: "Save, Lord; we are perishing"; Luke 8:24: "Master, Master, we are perishing.") Jesus calms the elements and stills the storm (4:39), and then turns to the disciples and reproaches them for failing in the hour of peril: "Why are you such cowards? Do you not yet have faith?" (The RSV translation of 4:40 is inadequate.) The disciples' reaction to Jesus' criticism is one of consternation and even fright: "And they were frightened with great fear." (The RSV translation of 4:41, "and they were filled with awe," gives the erroneous impression that the disciples were awestruck in view of Jesus' extraordinary powers.) Mark, far from depicting reverential disciples in awe of Jesus, gives us panic-stricken disciples who are frightened by Jesus' rebuke and ignorant as to his true identity: "Who then is this, that even the wind and the sea obey him?" (4:41).

In the initial event of the boat trip section Mark highlights the double motif of Jesus' power and the disciples' failure. From the very outset, therefore, the reader is sensitized to the crucial issue handled in this section: Will the disciples understand Jesus and the purpose of his journey or will they not?

The initial verse of the Gerasene exorcism (5:1–20) informs the reader that Jesus and the disciples have arrived at the other side of the lake (5:1). The setting of the exorcism, the most violent and massive of all the Gospel's exorcisms, is thus an area to the east of the Lake of Galilee. The incident has an unmistakable Gentile coloring. The unclean spirits enter a herd of swine, the symbol of Gentile uncleanliness. While there is no mention of a synagogue, reference is made in 5:20 to the Decapolis, a cluster of Hellenistic cities on the east bank of the Jordan river. We must conclude, therefore, that the incident of the Gerasene demoniac depicts a massive exorcism on Gentile land. By the drowning of the swine Gentile land is exorcised, that is, cleansed of Gentile pollution.

This cleansing of Gentile uncleanliness in turn gives us a clue to the purpose of the crossing of the lake. It signals not merely Jesus' authority over wind and water, but in the continuing gospel story Jesus' mastering of the elements facilitates passage to the Gentiles. In religious terms, the crossing symbolizes the opening of new frontiers and a breakthrough toward a new identity. But do the disciples understand this?

Why would Jesus perform an exorcism—and one of such massive proportions—upon arrival on Gentile territory? To fully understand this feature we must briefly flash back to an event in the first part of the Gospel. Immediately following the calling of the four disciples (1:16–20), we remember, Jesus had performed an exorcism in the synagogue of Capernaum as his first public act (1:21–28). If we keep this exorcism in the synagogue in mind, an overall logic, a pattern of correspondences, begins to emerge. Jesus opens his public activity with an exorcism in a Jewish setting. After the breakthrough toward the Gentiles on the eastern side of the lake, he does exactly what he had done on the Jewish side: he performs an exorcism. The massive proportions of that exorcism accord it a programmatic significance. Gentile territory is cleansed as a matter of principle, and Gentiles are acceptable in the Kingdom of God.

In 5:21 the reader recognizes an actual crossing of the lake. We are therefore back on what appears to be Jewish land. Both the raising of Jairus's daughter and the healing of a woman with an issue of blood are marked by Jewish symbols. Jairus is the ruler of a synagogue (5:22). The woman's duration of suffering is given as twelve years (5:25), and the daughter's age as twelve years (5:42). Reference to the synagogue and the number twelve, symbolic ultimately of the twelve tribes of Israel, are indicators of the Jewishness of the two events.

One further observes in the case of these two events a particular Markan technique of arranging story material. The author presents one part of the story of Jairus's daughter (5:21–24), then breaks it off and narrates the story of the hemorrhaging woman (5:25–34); after terminating the latter he continues the initial story and brings it to completion (5:35–42). By inserting the story of the hemorrhaging woman into that of Jairus's daughter, Mark achieves a desired narrative effect. The insertion dramatizes tension and focuses upon the miracle of the resurrection. When Jairus approaches Jesus, his daughter is still alive. She is near death, but there is still hope that she could be healed. Then Jesus allows himself to be distracted by the hemorrhaging woman and passes up the chance to rescue the girl from death. No sooner is the woman with an issue healed than the news arrives of the death of Jairus's daughter. Now it is in the face of death that Jesus performs not merely a healing but his greatest miracle on behalf of a human, the resurrection of a dead person.

The significance of the resurrection miracle is further emphasized by the fact that no one is allowed to witness the raising except the three chosen disciples, Peter, James, and John (5:37). These three are privileged to observe Jesus' authority over death. Having seen his power, they can and ought to know what kind of person Jesus is and what to expect of him.

We shall summarize the events observed up to this point. We saw Jesus proceeding from what turned out to be the Jewish side of the lake. On his arrival at the Gentile side he performed the most massive exorcism ever—as if to cleanse the Gentile land altogether. Then we observed him returning to the Jewish side and performing his greatest miracle ever—the resurrection of Jairus's daughter. There is a logic to these crossings and to the events before and after them. It is not the logic of a break with the Jewish side and an unswerving pull toward the Gentiles. Rather it is a logic which embraces both sides of the lake. The Jewish and the Gentile land are sanctioned, as if both belonged to the Kingdom of God.

ENDORSEMENT OF THE JEWS

After Mark has made the point of the inclusive nature of the Kingdom, he reports the rejection at Nazareth (6:1–6). Jesus enters his hometown (the RSV translation "his own country" is misleading), which must be Nazareth, since Jesus is the man from Nazareth (1:9). On the one hand the villagers cast doubt upon Jesus and dissociate themselves from him, while on the other hand Jesus breaks with them, citing the famous proverb of the prophet who is honored except in his own place (6:4). Specifically, the proverb legitimizes Jesus' estrangement from the village of Nazareth, from his relations in a broad sense, and from his own family. With minor exceptions, Jesus cannot honor Nazareth, its people, and his blood relatives with deeds of power (6:5). His very home and those who should be closest to him are thereby excluded from the campaign for the Kingdom of God. The attentive reader will connect this Nazareth rejection with the earlier incident when Jesus had relegated his own family to the outside (3:21, 31–35).

Immediately following the break with Nazareth and his own, Jesus initiates the mission of the Twelve (6:7–13, 30). He sends out the twelve disciples, giving them authority to do what he himself had been doing: to prepare for the Kingdom by preaching repentance, healing, and exorcising. When they return from their mission they return as apostles (6:30). This is with one possible exception (3:14) the only time Mark will call the disciples apostles. Henceforth he will continue to call them disciples. It was the nature of the missionary journey to initiate them into the nature of apostleship. While they are disciples in the presence of Jesus, they will become apostles apart from and in the absence of Jesus. The missionary journey has thus prepared the disciples for the future, when they will have to function as apostles in Jesus' absence.

Inserted into the missionary journey is the story of the death of John the Baptist (6:17–29). By now the reader is familiar with this Markan insertion technique and will recognize, in this case, the evangelist's intention to connect the mission of the Twelve and the death of John the Baptist. What could be the meaning of a synchronization of these two events? Two considerations will help us toward an answer. The first concerns the role of John the Baptist in the Markan Gospel. He is, we saw, depicted as the forerunner of Jesus. But in the Gospel John is a forerunner not merely in a temporal sense but also in an existential sense. He not only precedes Jesus temporally but he serves as a model for what will happen to Jesus. As John was "delivered up" to death (1:14), so will Jesus be "delivered up" to death (9:31; 10:33). The passion narrative of John the Baptist (6:17–29) can therefore be perceived as an anticipation of Jesus' own death, and the synchronization of John's death with the disciples' mission becomes intelligible as an analogy to Jesus' death and the beginnings of the apostolic mission. As John's death coincided with the sending out of the disciples-apostles, so will Jesus' death usher in the mission.

A second consideration concerns the didactic and prospective quality of the gospel narrative. The Markan Jesus all along his way shows and teaches the disciples (didactic quality) what they have to appropriate at some future point (prospective quality). Throughout the Gospel the disciples are being groomed so as to be able to assume apostolic responsibilities in the absence of Jesus. Anticipating his own destiny, Jesus prepares the disciples for the time when he will no longer be with them. They have participated in the journey toward the Gentiles—which should prepare them for their future mission. They have witnessed Jesus' power over death—which should give them a clue as to Jesus' dealing with his own death. They were present at Jesus' break with Nazareth (6:1)—which should caution them against founding their mission on those normally closest to Jesus. Finally, the disciples have been given a trial run of their mission in connection with the death of the forerunner—which should give them a clue as to the timing of their apostolic enterprise. They ought to go and stay with Jesus all the way, bury him just as John's disciples buried their master (6:29), and then undertake the mission among Jews and Gentiles alike. That much the disciples can and ought to know at this point in the gospel story.

The verses 6:31–33, setting the stage for the first feeding event, tell a complicated boat trip story. Crowded in by the people, Jesus and the disciples fetch the boat which is to take them to a quiet place. But the people on shore, watching their departure and anticipating their destination, run "on foot" (6:33) along the shore and arrive ahead of Jesus and the disciples at their landing place. This third voyage is therefore not a crossing of the lake but a change of place on its Jewish shoreline.

The feeding of the five thousand (6:34–44) is situated in a Jewish milieu, a fact corroborated by the reference to the twelve baskets (6:43). When Jesus sees the people, they appear to him "like sheep without a shepherd" (6:34). Their state of disorientation anticipates the kind of situation that would arise with Jesus' own death, when his prediction would be fulfilled: "I will strike the shepherd, and the sheep will be scattered" (14:27). It is in preparation for this leaderless condition that Jesus performs the feeding.

In reading the feeding story one should observe, as always in Mark, the role played by the disciples as much as that of Jesus. Their involvement in the feeding goes far beyond giving Jesus a helping hand. They are commissioned to feed the people (6:37), they are to look for food (6:38), they are instructed to make the

crowds settle down in order (6:39 is not adequately translated in
RSV), and they do feed the people, distributing the bread among
them (6:41). More than the disciples helping Jesus feed the
people, this is a case of Jesus showing the disciples how to feed
the people. It is not sufficient, therefore, to note that the feeding
story reports Jesus' feeding of the people. More specifically, we
must say, the Markan Jesus, in anticipation of a leaderless situation, places the disciples in charge over the Jewish part of the
community. But the attentive reader continues to wonder whether
the disciples truly understand the significance of this feeding.
Their motions to dismiss the people (6:35–36) and to buy bread
(6:37) suggest that initially they had no idea of what Jesus was
going to do. When they followed his instructions did they grasp
that they were put in the place of shepherds over the people?

ENDORSEMENT OF THE GENTILES

After the endorsement of the Jews one expects a similar event
on behalf of the Gentiles. The organization of the Gentiles first
requires another crossing of the lake. The story traditionally
called the walking on the water (6:45–52) enacts this second
boat trip, the fourth voyage altogether. There can be no doubt
that this time an actual crossing is reported. Verse 6:45 mentions
going "to the other side," and 6:53 announces the accomplished
passage. The first time Jesus and the disciples had crossed the
lake, we remember, Jesus had pioneered the breakthrough to the
Gentiles. This second time the disciples are urged to make it on
their own initiative. The first verb in 6:45 connotes the meaning
of urging, or forcing. Jesus "made them go," that is, he put
pressure on them to leave without his assistance. As was the case
the first time, the second passage is rough and the disciples fail
to overcome the adversity. When Jesus appears on the lake they
are terrified and take him for a ghost. But Jesus identifies himself, enters their boat, and the storm settles down. The disciples,
however, are in a state of utter perplexity, "for they did not
understand about the loaves; instead their heart was hardened"
(6:52). "The loaves" harks back to the feeding, and the disciples'
lack of understanding concerning the loaves confirms the reader's

suspicion that they had failed to grasp the meaning of the feeding event. Their hardening of heart is a deadly serious matter. (Neither Matthew nor Luke will accept this accusation leveled against the disciples.) In Jewish literature the hardening of heart intimates disobedience, loss of redemption, and even death. The accusation is all the more dramatic in Mark's Gospel because in 3:5 Jesus had charged his opponents with hardness of heart. By applying this very accusation now to the disciples, Mark has taken a decisive step toward identifying the disciples as Jesus' opponents.

After arrival on the Gentile side, Jesus performs a vast number of healings at Gennesaret (6:53–56). The reader will remember that the first landing on that side of the lake had issued in a massive exorcism. This second arrival is followed by healings. Jesus' activity among the Gentiles clearly parallels that among the Jews. On the Jewish side, we saw, Jesus' first deed of power had been the exorcism in the synagogue at Capernaum (1:21–28); it was immediately followed by the healing of Peter's mother-in-law (1:29–31). The point Mark is making seems obvious. By acting in parallel fashion on either side of the lake, the Markan Jesus accepts and sanctions both a Jewish and a Gentile constituency.

The author of the Markan Gospel feels and writes from a Jewish perspective. The integration of the Gentiles constitutes a difficult problem for him, which calls for special clarification. Before the acceptance of the Gentiles is formalized, the legal issue has to be settled. This is the function of the abolition of ritual taboos (7:1–23). The argument begins harmlessly enough with the issue of ritual washing before meals (7:1–5). But as it develops, the issue is radicalized to the point where all ritual cleanliness is under scrutiny. In the end the Markan Jesus overrules not merely the rules of ritual washing but all regulations pertaining to ritual cleanliness (7:15). A new morality of inward purity has replaced external purity.

In the context of the Gospel's story line the abolition of the ritual taboos breaks down the legal barrier which had stood in the way of accepting the Gentiles on their terms. What counts in the Kingdom of God is not Jewishness or Gentileness but the heart of the people. It is this new interiorization of morality which the disciples are invited to come to terms with. When in a private session, however, Jesus expresses his disappointment over the disciples' lack of perception (7:17–18) and then proceeds to give them further instructions (7:18–23), the nagging question arises again whether the disciples did this time or will ever understand Jesus and the nature of the Kingdom.

No sooner has Jesus legitimized what today we would call an open society than he further stretches its borderlines far to the north and away from the center of Jerusalem. In his dealing with the Syrophoenician woman (7:24–30) he pushes the new communal identity to its limits geographically, ethnically, and sexually. He journeys all the way up to the largely Gentile territory around Tyre (7:24)—geographical extension. His encounter there is with a Gentile person (7:26)—ethnic expansion. In effect he is helping two female sufferers, a mother and her daughter—sexual inclusiveness.

Jesus responds to the Syrophoenician woman's request to exorcise her daughter by raising the issue of the Jewish-Gentile priority. His statement, first feed the children and don't throw their food to the dogs, confirms the priority of the Jews. Clearly the children are meant to be the Jews, and the dogs stand for the Gentiles. Again we see the Gospel's author arguing from a basically Jewish perspective. Indeed his dramatization of the way of Jesus conforms precisely to this pattern: first to the Jews, then to the Gentiles. In principle the Kingdom is the prerogative of the Jews. But the Syrophoenician woman, surpassing the disciples in perception and determination, urges Jesus to extend his powers to her suffering daughter. In response Jesus heals the girl and in this way bestows his blessing upon the two Gentile women.

As yet no crossing back to the Jewish side has been reported. After the healing of the Gentile girl, Jesus undertakes a comprehensive journey covering predominantly Gentile land: the area of Tyre and Sidon in the north, touching on what must be the eastern shoreline of the lake, and the Decapolis to the southwest of the lake (7:31). It is presumably on this Gentile journey that Jesus performs the healing of the deaf-mute (7:32–37), his last

deed of power while on the Gentile side. The breakthrough toward the Gentiles, we notice again, is a burdensome matter, and
Mark's narrative argument is accordingly elaborate.

After a massive exorcism (5:1–20) and a vast number of healings (6:53–56) among Gentiles, an individual exorcism (7:24–30)
and an individual healing (7:32–37) in Gentile land, the time has
come for the formal ratification of the Gentile part of the community. The feeding of the four thousand (8:1–9), the expected
counterpart to the earlier feeding of the five thousand, constitutes this Gentile confirmation. This interpretation is demanded
both contextually and by at least one feature of the story proper.
Contextually, the Gospel's drama has been building up toward a
climactic feeding event ever since the second passage to the
eastern shore, and Jesus' wide-ranging journey (7:31) appears to
have concluded his mission among the Gentiles. As for a Gentile
identification signaled in the story itself, repeated reference to
the number seven (8:5, 6, 8), a number also which the disciples
themselves have to reiterate (8:5), is generally taken to symbolize
the Gentiles. From a Jewish or Jewish-Christian perspective,
seven is the number indicating wholeness, perfection, and uni-
versality. Not to be excluded is the possibility that Mark, by
emphasizing the number twelve in the Jewish feeding and seven
in the Gentile feeding, has a recollection of the early Christian
community at Jerusalem which—according to Luke—was presided
over by the leadership structure of the Twelve but also by a group
made up of seven Hellenists under the supervision of Stephen
(Acts 6:1–6).

As was the case in the first feeding, Jesus acts in the second
feeding also out of compassion and in response to the people's
needs (6:34; 8:2). Not unlike the first feeding, Jesus this second
time actively involves the disciples in the feeding event. He calls
the disciples (8:1), gives them the bread and the fish after the
blessing, and instructs them to distribute the food among the
people (8:6). In this manner the disciples are initiated into the
feeding of the Gentiles. Both their feeding of the Jews and their
feeding of the Gentiles should enlighten them with respect to
their own future roles and the kind of community for which they
were to carry responsibility.

The feeding is immediately followed by another boat trip (8:10), the fifth voyage altogether, but like the third trip not an actual crossing. We register a change of place on the Gentile shore. In this setting the Pharisees' request for a sign (8:11–12) will relate to the accomplished mission of the Gentiles. A heavenly miracle is to confirm Jesus' inclusion of the Gentiles. But Jesus refuses to give a sign, the implication being that he is the heavenly authenticated authority himself (1:11). He himself is the heavenly sign above which no sign can be given.

THE ISSUE OF THE ONE LOAF

Verse 8:13 indicates a crossing, the return trip back to the Jewish side. This sixth and last passage completes the itinerary, and completes it on a note of high drama. It is during this last crossing of the lake that the conflict between Jesus and the disciples reaches unprecedented heights, confirming the reader's suspicion that the disciples had failed to grasp the logic of Jesus' travels.

The confrontation between Jesus and the disciples (8:14–21), as this climactic event should be called, begins with the statement that the disciples had forgotten to take "loaves" with them on the trip. (The RSV rendering in 8:14 with "bread" is a mistranslation; the plural is crucial for an understanding of the plot.) While worrying about the absence of *loaves,* the disciples do as a matter of fact have *one loaf* with them in the boat (8:14). Yet again, in 8:16, they keep debating and deploring a lack of loaves. Their thinking moves on the material level of food shortage and supply. Recognizing their limited perception Jesus asks: "What are you discussing that you do not have loaves? Do you not yet perceive, do you not grasp?" (8:17). Theirs is a case of not seeing the forest for the trees. They ask for loaves, but they are in possession of one loaf, and still they cannot perceive the truth. The truth is what they have but cannot see. They have one loaf which embodies the oneness of Jews and Gentiles. This oneness Jesus had manifested during the boat trips. The loaf they have is symbolic of the unity of all. This is what the voyages were all about. Angered over the disciples' failure, Jesus now reiterates his

earlier charge of hardness of heart (8:17). The reader will remember that in 6:52 Mark had first used this very condemnation to characterize the disciples as Jesus' opponents (cf. 3:5).
This time, however, the hardness of heart accusation is reinforced
with that of blindness of eyes and deafness of ears: "Having
eyes do you not see, and having ears do you not hear?" (8:18).
This charge also resumes an earlier dramatic point in the Gospel.
In 4:11-12, we recall, Jesus had separated the Twelve and
"those about him" from outsiders, and characterized the latter as
people who "look and look, but do not see, and hear and hear,
but do not understand" (4:12). By applying this outsider char-
acterization now to the disciples, Mark has in effect cast them to
the outside. While the charge of hardness of heart puts the disciples into the role of opposition, that of blindness and deafness
reveals that they are about to forfeit their privileged position as
insiders. The followers are on the way of becoming opponents,
and the insiders the outsiders.

One last time Jesus reminds the disciples of the two pivotal
events they were privileged to witness and partake in during the
boat trips. Do they not remember the five loaves and the feeding
of the five thousand, and the seven loaves and the feeding of the
four thousand? He makes them repeat the symbolic numbers
which should have tipped them off: twelve and seven (8:19-20).
And again Jesus asks, "Do you still not understand?" (8:21).
On this unhappy note and with this question left unanswered,
the boat trips come to an end.

SUMMARY

Mark narrates in 4:35—8:21 the elementary story of the communal dimension of the Kingdom, divided into two ethnic halves
yet in the end united as one. To accomplish this unification,
Mark uses the symbols of the lake, which serves as a barrier
between the two sides; the two storm scenes, which dramatize
the difficulty concerning the Gentile inclusion; the territories on
either side, which signify Jewish and Gentile identities; the loaf
and the loaves, which indicate unity and the disciples' failure to
understand it; the boat, which functions as a vehicle of unifica-

tion; and six boat trips, which impose a comprehensive logic upon the whole section. The boat trips, alternating between the two sides and giving each side due blessing and respect, dramatize a unitive movement. What happens as a result of these voyages is that the lake loses its force as a barrier and is transformed into a symbol of unity, bridging the gulf between Jew and Gentile. There is only one loaf, not two and not many. The human condition is no longer definable in pairs of opposition; contradictions and hostilities are overcome. That is the fundamentally religious significance of the boat trip section. The Two are the One. The dimensions of the Kingdom are universal.

Mark's concern for unity and equality extends to his treatment of males and females. It is difficult to overlook his effort to place males and females on either side of the lake so as to assure their equal standing in the new community. On the Jewish side the evangelist tells of a father and the raising of his daughter (5:21–24, 35–42), as well as of the healing of a woman (5:25–34). On the Gentile side he gives an account of a mother and her daughter (7:24–30), and two additional accounts each dealing with a male sufferer (5:1–20; 7:32–37). Males and females on the Jewish and Gentile side are incorporated in the Kingdom of God.

Mark unifies and equalizes, but he does so at the expense of the disciples. It is the disciples (and not the Jews!) who in this section have emerged as the true opponents of Jesus. Their failure is epitomized in the concluding trip back to the Jewish side. The hardness of heart accusation, together with that of an entire lack of perception, reverses the disciples' earlier privileged insider status. They have failed to grasp the logic of Jesus' journey and are about to be an obstacle on the way to the Kingdom. The insiders have become opponents and outsiders.

The boat trip section leaves the reader with a question. Do the disciples understand or do they not understand the way of Jesus? As they embark together with Jesus on the road to Jerusalem, they leave without a proper understanding of the nature of the Kingdom and without memory of what Jesus instructed them to do and to be. This failure to understand the mission of Jesus is bound to have serious consequences, unless "they should turn again and be forgiven" (4:12).

3
The Suffering
of the
Son of Man

MARK 8:22—10:52

The central section of the Gospel (8:22—10:52) traces the way from Caesarea Philippi in the north to Bethsaida at the threshold of Jerusalem. While traveling this way Jesus prepares his disciples specifically for what is to happen after their arrival in Jerusalem. As a result the reader gains deeper insight into the person of Jesus and likewise into the nature of the disciples.

THE JOURNEY TO DEATH

We shall begin by observing the Markan construction of the way motif. Throughout the midsection our author has placed the clause "on the way." In part it is by means of this structuring device that Mark has sketched the journey of Jesus and his disciples. At the very outset (8:27) Jesus asks "on the way" the crucial question concerning his identity. The way motif is linked with the place of departure, Caesarea Philippi. (In Matthew and Luke the way motif is absent at this point.) This whole midsection of the Gospel concludes with the statement (10:52) that Bartimaeus, after having received sight, "followed him on the way." The way motif prepares for Jerusalem. (The motif is absent in Matthew and Luke.) In 9:33 Jesus asks his disciples what they had been discussing "on the way," and in 9:34 the reader is reminded that it had been "on the way" that the disciples were arguing over who was the greatest. The way motif is linked up with Capernaum. (The motif is absent in Matthew and Luke.) In 10:17 Mark uses literally the same phrase, "as he was setting out on his way." (The motif is absent in Matthew and Luke.) In 10:32, finally, the way motif is for the first time linked with Jerusalem: "and they were on the way, going up to Jerusalem." (The motif is absent in Matthew and Luke.)

It is fair to say that Mark has structured the central part of his Gospel with the way motif. At the outset, at the end, and at measured intervals in between he has introduced the "way signs" into this section, and each time they are absent in Matthew and in Luke. Mark, more so than Matthew and Luke, conceived of this part of the gospel in terms of a journey. Just as in the preceding section Mark organized the story around six boat trips, so he composed the Gospel's midsection along the six way references.

In addition to the way clauses, Mark has placed a comprehensive frame around the midsection. At the outset he reported the healing of the blind man of Bethsaida (8:22–26), and at the end, the healing of blind Bartimaeus (10:46–52). The whole section is thus framed by two stories each of which describes the opening of the eyes of a blind man. By framing the central section in such a manner, our author has given it a distinct interpretation. As the frame conditions the content, so do the framing stories cast interpretative light on the purpose of the journey. The opening of eyes is what Jesus does at the beginning and at the end of the way, and this is also what characterizes his relation with the disciples all along the way. To open the eyes of the disciples and make them see is the overriding purpose of the journey from Caesarea Philippi to Jerusalem. What Jesus does on behalf of the two blind men at the beginning and at the end, he tries to do on behalf of the disciples all the way through.

What is it that the Markan Jesus teaches his disciples on the way? What does he want them to see? There is one statement

Jesus repeats three times, and this reiteration informs the reader
of its crucial significance. While on the way to Jerusalem Jesus
predicts three times his imminent death and resurrection (8:31;
9:31; 10:33–34). These three so-called passion-resurrection predictions are not entirely identical, and biblical scholars evalu-
ate their subtle differences. In a general sense, however, each
passion-resurrection prediction conveys the same message: the
Son of man must die, and he will be resurrected after three days.
One further observes that the first part of these passion-resurrection sayings, which deals with suffering and death, is elaborated   – ✓
to a considerable extent, whereas the resurrection part constitutes a terse formula. There is great emphasis on Jesus' suffering:
his being rejected, delivered up into the hands of the establishment, tortured, and killed. The subsequent reference to his
resurrection after three days sounds almost anticlimactic.

Moreover each passion-resurrection prediction is articulated at
a different geographical place. The first prediction occurs in the
area of Caesarea Philippi (8:27), the second on the way through
Galilee (9:30), and the third while "going up to Jerusalem"
(10:32). In this manner Mark has carefully integrated the passion-resurrection predictions into the journey motif. Three times,
and at three different places on the way, Jesus speaks solemnly
of his violent death and also of his resurrection.

The three passion-resurrection predictions are clearly intended
for the disciples. Yet the attentive reader will recognize Mark's
special handling of the audience. The first passion-resurrection
prediction is directed to the disciples at large (8:31). The second
prediction is addressed to the disciples (9:31) but specifically in-
terpreted to the Twelve (9:35). The third prediction is exclusively
spoken to the Twelve (10:32). According to Mark's conception
the disciples comprise the larger body of followers while the
Twelve form the leadership group. At certain points in the gospel
story Mark will single out the Twelve (or the Three: Peter, James,
and John) to convey a message of special significance to these
future leaders of the community. By reiterating the passion-
resurrection predictions three times and by bringing the focus
increasingly on the Twelve, Mark has made his point very clear.

That Jesus is going to Jerusalem in order to die and be resurrected is what the disciples, and above all the Twelve, have to learn on the way to Jerusalem.

Three times and at three different "stations of the cross" Jesus initiates the disciples, and more and more the Twelve, into the purpose of their pilgrimage to Jerusalem. He spares no efforts to open their eyes and make them see the meaning of his life. He is going to be a suffering and rejected person, tormented, spat upon, and killed. But he will overcome death and rise after three days. That much the Twelve can and must know. By the time they arrive in Jerusalem, they can and ought to be prepared for what will happen. There will be no excuse if they do not know. Jesus has made every effort to open their eyes.

At this point in the gospel story the reader is fully aware of serious problems concerning the disciples and their perception of Jesus' message and mission. Will they finally learn to see the truth, or will they remain blind to the realities of Jesus' life and death? The reader learns the answer to this question by observing the disciples' responses to the three passion-resurrection predictions.

CONFRONTATION BETWEEN PETER AND JESUS

The first passion-resurrection prediction (8:31) is part of a larger story complex which is traditionally called Peter's confession. We shall in the following demonstrate the inadequacy of this traditional title and suggest the more appropriate one of the confrontation between Jesus and Peter (8:27-33). The incident commences with Jesus' question concerning his identity (8:27). Various identifications are suggested (8:28). Then Jesus asks the disciples about their opinion, and it is in response to this question that Peter, acting as their spokesman, makes his so-called confession: "You are the Christ" (8:29). At this point the reader must assume that Peter's answer is correct, hence a true confession. This must be assumed if only for the reason that Mark appears to have authenticated the Christ confession with the very first verse of the Gospel: "The beginning of the gospel of Jesus Christ, the Son of God" (1:1).

However, the correctness of Peter's so-called confession can only be maintained if one stops reading at this point. If one continues reading to the end, the certainty of Peter's confession rapidly diminishes. Jesus' reaction to Peter's statement seems strange: "And he rebuked them to tell no one about him" (8:30; the RSV rendering with "charged them" is not true to the original). As it stands, the verse is ambiguous and leaves the option open as to whether Peter was right or wrong. On the one hand the verse could mean that Jesus wanted the disciples to keep silent because Peter's confession is correct. This is not as absurd as it may seem, since earlier in the Gospel Jesus had prohibited the demons from making his identity known, although they had recognized him (1:34; 3:11–12). The possibility exists that Peter and the disciples are to protect the incognito of Jesus precisely because they perceive his true identity. On the other hand the verse could mean that they are rebuked to keep silent because they have the wrong understanding of Jesus. The question raised in the reader's mind by 8:30 is therefore this: Is Peter's confession to be suppressed because it is correct, or because it is incorrect and possibly made under false preconceptions? The reader, anticipation aroused and curiosity mounting, is strongly motivated to keep on reading. Verse 8:30 is definitely not the end of this particular story.

In 8:31 Mark presents Jesus' first passion-resurrection prediction: "The Son of man must suffer many things, and be rejected by the elders and the chief priests and the scribes, and be killed, and after three days rise again." This statement Jesus makes "plainly" (8:32), that is, without imposing silence upon the disciples. In the context, this is now Jesus' confession of his identity in response to Peter's confession. At this point the reader could still assume that Jesus' confession is in accord with Peter's confession and Peter's confession conforms to Jesus' confession. But this is the last time in that story that Peter's confession can escape censure. In 8:32, in the wake of Jesus' confession, Peter proceeds to rebuke Jesus. Now it is unmistakably plain. If Peter rebukes Jesus on the heels of his (Jesus') confession, then Peter disagrees with Jesus' confession, and Peter's Christ confession cannot have been in harmony with Jesus' suffering Son of man confession. Whatever Peter's concept of Christ, it is in conflict with Jesus' concept of Christ.

The conflict between Jesus and Peter is all the more dramatic if one remembers that in the Markan Gospel the word *rebuke* is a technical term connoting exorcism language. When earlier Jesus rebuked the unclean spirit (1:25), he identified and treated him as a demonic force. The threefold rebuking in our story conjures up a demonic milieu and suggests that each of the two protagonists treats the other as a satanic personality. Jesus rebukes Peter and the disciples in view of Peter's so-called confession (8:30). Next Peter rebukes Jesus following his (Jesus') Son of man confession (8:32). The story climaxes with Jesus again rebuking Peter, now identifying him logically in the context of their mutual rebuking as Satan (8:33).

In 8:27–33 Mark proves himself a master of the dramatic art. The scene of confrontation between Jesus and Peter is a skillfully designed and circumspectly plotted dramatic scene. Mark sets it up in such a way that the reader almost instinctively identifies with Peter and his Christ confession. He teases the reader, as it were, into accepting Peter's confession at face value. But then Mark unfolds the drama by emphasizing increasingly the negative aspects of Peter until in the end he shatters the veracity of Peter's confession and wrecks the reader's identification with Peter. The scene culminates in the highly dramatic confrontation between Peter and Jesus, each rebuking the other and Peter in the end being exposed as Satan. In the Gospel Peter is the only human being who is identified, and identified by Jesus, as a satanic person. It is overwhelmingly clear: Peter's confession has not been the correct confession. To call 8:27–33 the story of Peter's confession, as we Christians have done in the past, is to completely misread the Markan dramatization. Peter's so-called confession is only the initial stage in a dramatically developed story which culminates in Jesus refuting Peter and thereby discrediting his confession. This is why we must call Mark 8:27–33 the confrontation between Jesus and Peter.

THE DISCIPLES' LACK OF PERCEPTION

The confrontation between Jesus and Peter discloses the discipleship failure in connection with the first passion-resurrection prediction. While in the wake of the first prediction Peter is exposed as Satan, it is after the second prediction that the disciples are convicted of nonperception. The second prediction (9:31) is immediately followed by the succinct comment, "But they did not understand the saying, and they were afraid to ask him" (9:32). These two motifs, lack of perception and fearful inhibition to ask for an explanation, reinforce each other and strengthen the case of the disciples' dilemma. If they do not understand what is being said but are afraid to find out, they will be locked ever more deeply into ignorance.

As if the reader is not already sufficiently mindful of the disciples' inadequacy, Mark continues to accentuate their failure as followers of Jesus. In 9:33–34 one learns that personal power and prestige is the disciples' favorite topic of discussion. Who is the greatest among them? This is not, as far as Mark is concerned, conduct becoming a disciple of Jesus. Jesus has twice announced his imminent suffering, torture, and death. The disciples' response to the second prediction was lack of understanding and fear. Next they discuss among themselves who is the greatest. In the face of Jesus' imminent crucifixion their discussion reveals a profoundly tactless attitude. Is it possible to highlight the disaster of the disciples more emphatically?

The disciples' passion for power brings back to mind Peter's satanic confession. Peter made his confession "not on the side of God, but of men" (8:33) because it implied the negation of a suffering Christ. The disciples' personal ambitions in the face of Jesus' pronouncement of his death likewise reflect an attachment to a Messiah who is beyond suffering and death. Peter and the disciples appear to derive their personal identities from a messianic concept of power and glory. Or perhaps more to the point, it is

out of a preoccupation with power and prestige that they invoke
a Messiah of power, hence turning a deaf ear to Jesus' passion-
resurrection predictions.

Jesus' reaction to the disciples' obsession with power and
prestige is highly significant. It comes in 9:35, a most unusual
verse (absent in both Matthew and Luke): "And he sat down,
called the Twelve, and said to them, 'If anyone wants to be first,
he must be last of all and a servant of all.' " There are two remarkable aspects to this verse. First, the Markan Jesus singles
out the Twelve. What he says is personally addressed to the
twelve leaders. Second, Jesus tells the Twelve that the first must
be the last. It is noteworthy that Jesus does not sound the well-
known reversal theme: the first shall be the last and the last
shall be first. Rather verse 9:35, spoken to the Twelve, states
simply that the first must be the last and serve. The term *first*
suggests the issue of priority, power, and authority. What is
under attack is the concept of authority as it was entertained by
the Twelve. The disciples' discussion about the greatest among
them revealed a hierarchical understanding of leadership. This
the Markan Jesus challenges. There is no place in the Kingdom
of God for a hierarchically organized leadership structure. Genuine authority is assumed by serving the people, all the people,
not by lording over them. Above all, authority means to show
concern for the little ones, the children, those who have least
power of all (9:36–37). This concept of power in service must
now be understood by the Twelve. As they approach Jerusalem
they ought to prepare themselves for the exercise of power in
service and stop thinking as if they were to become the leaders
of a new establishment.

The third passion-resurrection prediction, we remember, is
specifically directed to the Twelve (10:32–34). There can be no
doubt as to Jesus' supreme efforts to initiate the disciples, and
especially the Twelve, into his identity as a suffering, crucified,
and rising Messiah. The Twelve more than anyone else are
thoroughly prepared for what is going to happen in Jerusalem.
Yet again the announcement of suffering and death falls on deaf
ears. It is met with the request expressed by James and John for

positions of power (10:35–45). These sons of Zebedee, who together with Peter form the privileged triumvirate among the Twelve, ask for future "cabinet" positions in the face of Jesus' third and last passion-resurrection prediction on the threshold of Jerusalem. The supreme irony of their request cannot escape the reader who is familiar with the gospel story. The expressly stated wish, "to sit one at your right and one at your left, in your glory" (10:37), provokes Jesus' allusive remark, "You do not know what you are asking" (10:38). What in fact James and John are asking for is not ranks of power but a place in the shadow of death. At the crucifixion two outlaws will in effect assume the positions James and John had requested, "one at his right hand and one at his left" (15:27). Again one must wonder whether it is possible to underscore any more emphatically the complete misunderstanding on the part of the disciples, and especially of the Twelve, and most particularly of Peter, James, and John.

Apart from articulating his own future destiny in the three passion-resurrection predictions, Jesus also spells out the nature and conditions of discipleship in unequivocally plain words. Provided the disciples understand the mission of Jesus, his discipleship message will also make sense to them, because discipleship in Mark is closely fashioned after the model of the suffering Jesus. If this is understood, then the gist of the discipleship message does not come as a surprise. There can be little doubt regarding the essence of discipleship, as far as Mark is concerned. To follow Jesus means to deny oneself, to be the first in service and the last in power, to show a willingness to suffer— even to the point of losing one's life and drinking the cup that Jesus drinks (8:34–38; 10:42–45).

It is sometimes claimed that religion is a classic case of an escape from the realities of life, a denial of the brutalities of suffering and of our common destiny of death. Whoever makes such claims must not be familiar with the documents of the Old and New Testaments. Both deal extensively with the suffering of the people, the death of the just ones, and the seeming triumph of evil. The point could well be made that many of the biblical traditions in Judaism and Christianity struggle with the fundamental issues of human life: the suffering of the innocent, the destruction of individual and collective life, the annihilation of cities and civilizations, the overpowering force of evil, and man's alienation from himself and from God.

The Gospel of Mark serves as an example of deliberate integration of the realities of suffering and death. Mark traces the life of Jesus from a distinct philosophical viewpoint, or better perhaps, he derives a particular philosophy from the life of Jesus: there is no reward without toil and pain, and there can be no success without the suffering that precedes it. It may well be the single most important message the author wishes to convey: there is no life without death, and no Easter without crucifixion. The Markan emphasis lies heavily on the period of suffering and the crucifixion. He does not focus on Easter itself. The passion-resurrection predictions, we saw, elaborate the aspect of death more than that of the resurrection. The resurrected Jesus, we shall see, never makes an appearance in the Gospel of Mark. The discipleship sayings, we remember, are modeled after the suffering Jesus who is on his way to the cross. Discipleship is not derived from the glorified Jesus. Indeed, the Markan Jesus himself is not basking in his resurrection glory but serving on behalf of others and giving his life as a ransom for many. To put the matter frankly, Mark is not saying that a Christian life requires rebirth in the resurrection glory of the risen Lord. For Mark, to be a Christian means to follow Jesus on his way; to drink the cup of suffering; to be concerned with the salvation of others, and less—if at all—with one's own life and well-being.

Throughout the midsection of the Gospel Mark spares no effort to illustrate the persistent and incorrigible failure of the disciples, the Twelve, and the triumvirate. With methodical precision the evangelist has each passion-resurrection prediction evolve into a clear case of a discipleship misconception. Jesus speaks of his suffering and death; the disciples dream of personal power and success. They hear only what they want to hear, not what Jesus says. Peter, the leader, stands exposed as Jesus' satanic opponent. James and John, members of the triumvirate, calculate a splendid future for themselves, revealing a state of mind that is offensive even to the other ten (10:41). The disciples are incapable of exorcising an epileptic boy (9:14–29; cf. 9:18, 28), yet shortly thereafter John has the nerve to obstruct the healings of an exorcist who, while not one of the disciples, performs successfully in the name of Jesus. John's action promptly draws a reprimand from Jesus (9:38–41). Jesus advises the Twelve to be accepting toward children (9:35–37), but soon afterwards the disciples rebuke children, rejecting their membership in the new community. Again Jesus voices strong objections to the disciples' concept of the Kingdom of God (10:13–16). When Jesus declares the giving of all earthly possessions to the poor a precondition for entrance into the Kingdom (10:17–22), Peter confidently announces that this is just what he and his fellow disciples had done (10:28). But Jesus reminds him that such selfless giving will only be rewarded "with persecutions" (10:29–30), and that the new fellowship will come in such a way that "many that are first will be last, and the last first" (10:31). Whenever the disciples, the Twelve, or members of the triumvirate make an appearance in the midsection of the Gospel, they appear almost without exception either in overt or in covert conflict with Jesus.

THE GLORY OF THE SON OF GOD

There is yet one more event which deserves our attention. Following his confrontation with Peter (8:27–33) Jesus announces the conditions for discipleship (8:34-38) and his own future coming (9:1), and immediately thereafter takes Peter, James, and John up on a high mountain. It is on this mountain that he appears to the three disciples in a transformed state, and a heavenly voice identifies him as Son of God. In a number of ways this transfiguration of Jesus (9:2–8) forms the central scene of the whole Gospel. Structurally, in terms of number of verses, it stands almost exactly at midpoint in the gospel story. It constitutes the only "high mountain" scene in the Gospel. Outside of baptism this is the only time the life of Jesus is marked by divine intervention in visible and audible terms. There will be no

divine intervention at Jesus' passion and crucifixion. The literary
critic will call this transfiguration story the *scene of recognition*. At one point in a novel or drama or movie the author lets
the reader or viewer have a glimpse of the protagonist's full
identity, intimating thereby the final outcome of the story. The
transfiguration (not Peter's so-called confession!) is this scene
of recognition. For a brief moment Jesus is revealed to the three
witnesses as the Son of God in full glory.

It proves helpful to observe precisely at what point in the
dramatic development Mark places this scene of recognition. It
comes after Jesus has demonstrated his power over the demonic
forces, after he has outlined the communal profile of the Kingdom of God, after his first passion-resurrection prediction, and
after his first reference to his future coming in power. In short,
the scene of recognition is not presented until all the crucial
identifications of Jesus have been given: figure of power over
evil and death, founder of the new community, man of suffering
and death, victor over death who will come at some future time.
All these identifications are involved in the heavenly Son of
God declaration. This means that at this point in the Gospel's
story Jesus will yet have to go through suffering and death, and
will yet have to rise before he can appear as Son of God in full
glory. The transfiguration scene is therefore to be understood
as a preview, granted to the three chosen disciples, of Jesus' full
identity as Son of God, an identity which is yet to be fully
materialized through suffering and rising.

Do the three disciples understand this matter? Mark did not
hesitate to introduce even into the pivotal recognition scene
the motif of discipleship misconception. In 9:5 Peter suggests that
Jesus let them build booths, three altogether, one for Jesus, one
for Moses, and one for Elijah. Immediately following this pro-
posal one reads that, out of fear, Peter did not know what to
say. This verse 9:6, not unlike 9:32, displays the motifs of lack of
perception and fear, which in this combination reinforce the
failure of Peter. When he suggests to build booths he does not
know what he is saying, while fear prevents him from learning
the true meaning of the transfiguration. But Peter is not alone in

being convicted of ignorance. Mark takes care to implicate all three disciples: "For *he* did not know what to say, for *they* were exceedingly afraid" (9:6).

What is the nature of the disciples' misunderstanding in the transfiguration scene? By suggesting that they build booths, Peter wants to arrest and make a present reality of what was only meant to be a preview of the future. Because his gaze is fixed on the present and on present fulfillment, he desires to perpetuate the transfiguration glory. He cannot understand that Jesus will yet have to pass through suffering and death before he is Son of God for all to see. This attitude conforms well with what we already know of the disciples' craving for power and Peter's earlier objection to Jesus' first passion-resurrection prediction. They desire a shortcut to the Kingdom of God by eliminating the dimension of suffering and death. The Markan Jesus by contrast not only postpones fulfillment but insists on an irrevocable connection between true life and death on the cross. The glory of the transfiguration will not be consummated except through the agony on the cross.

SUMMARY

The reader may want to recollect the total construction of this central section of the Gospel: At the beginning and at the end Mark has placed a story dealing with the healing of a blind man. These framing stories signify the purpose of Jesus' journey from Caesarea Philippi to Jerusalem. As Jesus traveled his way he tried to open the eyes of the disciples first and foremost to the reality of his suffering, dying, and rising. By now the reader who has traveled along the way has come to the realization that the disciples have remained blind. The net result of this journey is not the opening of their eyes, but their incorrigible blindness. They have remained ignorant of the purpose of Jesus' mission, and for this reason cannot occupy the place and fulfill the function that was destined for them.

The reader who has reached this conclusion is compelled to take yet another look at Mark's framing composition: The disci-

ples do not see, but the two blind men at the beginning and at
the end do see. The whole section concludes with the statement
that Bartimaeus "followed him on the way" (10:52). The disciples who were on the inside and received Jesus' private instructions fail to see. The two on the outside, not disciples and not
privileged with personal instructions, nevertheless see, and
Bartimaeus follows on the way. The contrast Mark dramatizes
in this midsection of his Gospel is one of seeing versus nonseeing
and outsiders versus insiders. The two men who had been on the
outside turn out to be insiders while the disciples, the orginal insiders, are in the process of the journey relegated to the outside.

That in the last analysis is the disturbing but profoundly religious truth Mark conveys in the central section of his Gospel:
those who are closest to Jesus and claim to know best of all may
be furthest from the truth, while those who are spatially and
temporally removed from Jesus may spiritually and in the conduct of their lives be very close to him.

4
The End
of the
Temple

MARK 11:1—13:37

What gives focus to the section 11:1—13:37 is Jesus' dealings with the temple of Jerusalem. Three times, on three successive days, his entry into Jerusalem amounts to a journey into the temple. On the third day in the temple he delivers a series of speeches against the authorities, then exits the temple and immediately predicts its downfall.

FIRST JOURNEY TO THE TEMPLE

Upon arrival at the outskirts of Jerusalem Jesus and his disciples settle down at a place near the Mount of Olives (11:1), opposite the temple mountain. That location will serve them as a kind of base from which they undertake their temple journeys. It is from this place also that Jesus and his disciples prepare for what is commonly designated the triumphal entry into Jerusalem. As we have observed before, however, traditional titles placed over Gospel stories can be misleading. In the Gospel of Mark we do not find the Jerusalem population cheering and applauding Jesus at his entrance into the city. The people who hail Jesus are not the citizens of Jerusalem but "those who went before and those who followed" (11:9), that is, primarily the disciples and those who joined them on the way to Jerusalem. The acclamation (11:1–10) takes place on the way from the Mount of Olives to the city. It is only after the acclamation that Jesus enters the city itself, unapplauded and without public recognition (11:11).

The reader who has followed the narrative logic of Mark will be struck by the wording of the acclamation. In the words of his followers, Jesus is welcome as the inaugurator of "the kingdom of our father David" (11:10). Clearly what they have in mind is the restoration in power and glory of the Davidic kingdom on Mount Zion in Jerusalem (Amos 9:11; Isa. 9:6–7). But is it in Mark the mission of Jesus to fulfill his followers' conventional hopes of Davidic messianism? Is the Kingdom of God Jesus came to announce (1:15) identical with the kingdom of father David which the followers expect Jesus to bring? Do they celebrate on the way to the city the Jesus who had foretold his suffering and death in Jerusalem? Is he who rides on a colt "on which no one ever sat" (11:2) the expected Davidic Messiah? Once we have pursued questions along this line, it will dawn on us that in the context of Mark's story the acclamation scene is one of supreme irony. It is Jesus' followers who continuing to mistake his identity turn his journey to Jerusalem into a triumphal celebration. Those who acclaim Jesus' Davidic messiahship perpetuate an attitude shown earlier by the refusal to listen to the passion-resurrection predictions. As far as the followers are concerned, Jesus enters Jerusalem in order to establish the Kingdom in power. That is cause for celebration. As far as Jesus is concerned, he enters into suffering and death. He will not be King until he is nailed to the cross.

Jesus' first entry into Jerusalem is aimed at the temple (11:11). The temple, not the city as such, is of interest to him. He makes a survey of the temple, then leaves for the place from which they had departed. The Twelve are made to witness his solitary inspection of the temple. What they observe is hardly a triumphal entry. Jesus is neither recognized in the streets of Jerusalem nor installed in the temple as Davidic Messiah. His visit to the temple is not even associated with prayer and worship. He merely looks at everything in the temple, then leaves at nightfall. Can this be the Davidic Messiah who is to fulfill the hopes and aspirations of Mount Zion, the temple mountain of Jerusalem? What begins to surface in this strange and uniquely Markan verse 11:11 is Jesus' strained relationship with the temple and the temple mount. The temple will not be "his place," let alone the site of universal salvation.

SECOND JOURNEY AND TEMPLE DISQUALIFICATION

Before we give an account of Jesus' second day in the temple we must look at the Markan composition of 11:12-22. We observe that the story traditionally called the cleansing of the temple (11:15-19) is enclosed by the two parts of a story dealing with a fig tree. In 11:12-14 Mark reports Jesus' cursing of the fig tree; it is followed in 11:15-19 by the so-called cleansing story; in 11:20-22 the reader learns of the final outcome of the fig tree. A number of times already we had occasion to draw the reader's attention to the evangelist's favorite technique of framing one story by another one. In the present case the so-called story of the cleansing of the temple is framed by the fig tree story. By means of this specific framing arrangement (fig tree–"cleansing"–fig tree) Mark signals some kind of connection between fig tree and temple. That much the experienced reader of the Gospel can know by observing Mark's compositional technique.

Jesus' second day in the temple begins with the fig tree episode. On the way from "his place" in Bethany to Jerusalem Jesus becomes hungry. He sees a fig tree in full foliage, but as he approaches the tree he finds nothing but leaves. Apparently angered by the lack of fruit, Jesus expresses the desire that no one may ever eat again from it. Thus far the story is perfectly intelligible. The difficulty comes with the last clause of 11:13. Jesus finds no fruit "because it was not the right time for figs." That does not seem to make sense. Why condemn the tree if it is not the proper time for bearing fruit? The term inadequately translated in the RSV with "season" gives the clue to the puzzle. It is not a botanical term indicating the season for figs but a religious term denoting the time of the Kingdom of God. Indeed it is precisely the term Mark had used in Jesus' programmatic message announcing the "right time" of the Kingdom of God (1:14–15). By introducing this loaded religious term into the fig tree story Mark gives it a religious dimension. Jesus' encounter with the fig tree signifies more than the barrenness of a tree. The absence of "the right time for figs," we shall see, suggests the absence of the right time of the Kingdom. The disciples, Mark hastens to add (11:14), hear Jesus condemn the tree. They are placed in a position to draw the appropriate lesson from the barrenness of the fig tree.

Jesus' second journey into Jerusalem is again aimed at the temple (11:15). Mark reports two actions undertaken by Jesus at his second temple visit. First he disrupts the business transactions and ejects the tradespeople from the temple (11:15). Most readers, familiar with this story from childhood, are accustomed to placing this event in the forecourt of the temple. Yet Mark speaks only of the temple, never of the forecourt. What Jesus does and says on his second visit to the temple, he does and says in the temple, and it has a bearing on the temple. Specifically, his first action undercuts the material, financial side of the temple. The second action undertaken by Jesus in the temple is to prohibit people from carrying "anything" through the temple (11:16). The original Greek word for "anything" (mistranslated in the RSV) is *vessel*. Jesus would not allow anyone to carry a vessel through the temple. The reference to vessel in a temple story suggests a cultic dimension. By forbidding people to carry cultic objects through the temple, Jesus puts an end to the religious practices of the temple. To sum up, Jesus' two actions are tantamount to the shutting down of the business and religious functions of the temple. One must wonder whether this can truly be called a cleansing of the temple.

While still in the temple Jesus engages in teaching: "My house shall be called a house of prayer for all the nations; but you have made it a den of outlaws" (11:17). Implied in this statement is a twofold critique of the temple. First, the temple has served the special interests of one people. It shall be open to all the people. Second, the temple has become a haven for outlaws. Within the bounds of the story "outlaws" will refer to the money-changers and tradespeople who violated the sanctity of the holy place. But the Greek word for "outlaw" also has a special political meaning. It refers to political activists who entered Jerusalem from the country and turned the temple into a base for anti-Roman activities. At the peak of the Roman-Jewish War (A.D. 66–74) the temple was converted into a Zealotic fortress. The temple Jesus envisages is a house of prayer—not of business transactions or military action—and open to all the nations. Jesus' ideal of the house of God brings to mind his boat trips on and across the Lake of Galilee, and his breakthrough toward the Gentiles. There exists an unmistakable connection between the ecumenical community in the north and Jesus' vision of the "house of prayer for all the nations." The Jewish-Gentile community in the north has been purged by Jesus of evil forces, while the temple stands condemned of corruption by trade and politics. Had the disciples grasped Jesus' Jewish-Gentile mission in the north, they would now after Jesus' condemnation of the temple understand where the "house of prayer for all the nations" was to be and where it was not to be.

Jesus' teaching in the temple runs into the opposition of the temple authorities. The chief priests and scribes, determined to kill Jesus, seek a way of carrying out their plan (11:18). Not since the Pharisaic and Herodian plot was reported in 3:16 has Mark made it so brutally plain that the opponents are out to take the life of Jesus. But it is noteworthy that our evangelist distinguishes carefully between the temple establishment, which desires to destroy Jesus, and the masses of the people who are impressed by his teaching (11:18; 12:12, 37). In the evening of the second day Jesus and his disciples leave Jerusalem, presumably to return to Bethany at the Mount of Olives.

On the morning of the third day on the way back into the city, Jesus and his disciples again pass by the fig tree. It is obvious to them that the tree is withered "from the roots up" (11:20). Peter, the spokesman, remembers Jesus' earlier words of condemnation and points out the dead tree to him (11:21). Jesus responds with mysterious words of mountain-moving faith, prayer, and forgiveness. While the disciples should realize that the dead tree was shown to them in close connection with Jesus' temple visits, they must also remember that it does not spell the end of the way. Faith (5:36; 9:23), prayer (9:29; 14:38), and forgiveness (2:5, 10)—with one exception (3:28–30)—are the hallmarks of the new community.

One last time we must remember Mark's framing arrangement in terms of the fig tree–temple–fig tree. The framing stories concerning the fig tree interpret the temple story. Accordingly, the tree illustrates the temple, and the dead tree symbolizes the death of the temple. As the tree has withered "from the roots up," so is the temple adjudged by Jesus to be beyond hope. The hope Jesus encourages does not point to the temple but rather to the new fellowship in the Kingdom of God. The "right time" of the Kingdom, however, is not to be in the temple, the traditional seat of Davidic aspirations. For all these reasons it is misleading to call Mark 11:15–19 the cleansing of the temple. Cleansing implies that the temple has been reformed so as to function in a purified, new fashion. Mark's framing composition (11:12–25), however, dramatizes Jesus' disqualification of the Temple. Far from living up to expectations associated with the temple, Jesus makes "his place" at the Mount of Olives, opposite the temple mount, and journeys back and forth. He takes a stand outside, from which he turns against the temple.

THIRD JOURNEY AND TEMPLE SPEECHES

The third journey into Jerusalem ends once again in the temple (11:27). Jesus spends his last day in the temple (11:27; 12:35, 41; 13:1) as a teacher (12:14–15, 19, 32, 35, 38) who lectures on a number of controversial topics. He teaches with authority, holding up his own authority over against that of the temple and its authorities.

On the day after Jesus' temple disqualification the custodians of the temple—the high priests, scribes, and elders—ask him in the temple the question about authority (11:27–33): "By what authority are you doing these things?" (11:28). In the thorough-going temple context "these things" can only refer back to Jesus' condemnation of the temple. Who gave him the authority to do what he did in and to the center of religious life? Jesus deflects their question toward the issue of John's baptism. Was it "from heaven or from men?" (11:30). The reader knows that precisely at baptism Jesus was authorized by the heavenly voice. But the authorities, torn between unbelief and fear of the people, fail to answer Jesus' question. As a consequence their own question likewise remains unanswered.

Next Jesus takes the initiative and tells the temple authorities the parable of the wicked tenants (12:1–12), a harsh rebuke in allegorical language of those in charge of the temple. The tenants, placed in custody of the vineyard, are implicated in the murders of the servants sent to receive their rightful produce. In the end the tenants even kill the "beloved son" (12:6), "the heir" (12:7) to the vineyard. In punishment for their crimes the tenants will be destroyed; the vineyard will be given to others and Jesus will become its cornerstone. Upon hearing this story the temple authorities are enraged, "because they perceived that he had told the parable against them" (12:12). They were themselves compared to the murderous tenants who will suffer the loss of the temple. With this parable Jesus has set himself up as the cornerstone of the new temple, the Kingdom of God, which how-ever is not synonymous with the old temple but antithetical to it.

After Jesus' rupture with the temple authorities, the latter de-part from the temple but continue to operate in the background. They commission some Pharisees and Herodians to catch Jesus in his temple teaching. The question concerning tribute to Caesar (12:13–17), "Is it lawful to pay taxes to Caesar or not?" (12:14), is a profoundly sensitive question. It is brilliantly designed to implicate Jesus as a violent revolutionary, because it was by refusing to pay the imperial taxation that Israel later entered into the revolutionary War against Rome which resulted in the Jewish defeat and the destruction of the temple. Jesus' well-known

answer rejects any violent Zealotic insinuations: one may serve
God as well as Caesar. The Kingdom of God, while opposed by
the religious establishment, can coexist with the Roman power
structure.

The Sadducees' question concerning the resurrection (12:18–27)
marks yet another stage in the struggle between temple authorities and Jesus, who has declared himself above and against the
temple. They are the established temple aristocracy, and the
temple forms their base of power. By condemning the temple
Jesus had posed a threat to the Sadducean power center. On the
premise "that there is no resurrection" (12:18) they retaliate by
trying to convince Jesus of the absurdity of belief in the resurrection. That challenge goes to the core of Jesus' authority, because he has predicted his own resurrection three days after his
death. Jesus disproves the Sadducees by reference to the Scripture they hold in high esteem. According to Scripture God is a
God of the living, not of the dead.

A scribe in sympathy with Jesus' teaching asks the question
about the great commandment (12:28–34). Jesus cites the opening line of a noted Jewish prayer: "Hear, Israel, the Lord our
God is one Lord" (12:29). Implied in this prayer is a critique of
the temple which has failed to serve the needs of all the people.
The oneness of God demands the oneness of "all the nations"
(11:17). Rooted in this principle of the unity of God is the double
commandment of the love of God and love of neighbor (12:30–
31); it overrules all other laws and regulations (12:31). It provides the scriptural justification for Jesus' own life, for his repeal
of the law on his Galilean journeys, for his creation of the oneness
of the people during the crossings of the lake, for his death as
"a ransom for many" (10:45) announced on the way to Jerusalem,
and for his judgment upon the temple enacted on his temple
trips. In short, the double commandment constitutes the article
of faith for the new fellowship in the Kingdom. The scribe embraces Jesus' norm, explicating it over and against the temple's
"burnt offerings and sacrifices" (12:33), whereupon Jesus confirms that he is "not far from the Kingdom of God" (12:34).

Shortly before his final departure from the temple, Jesus clarifies the issue of his Davidic identity which had been pending ever since he and the disciples had approached Jerusalem, the city of David. Is he or is he not the Davidic Messiah? Jesus relates the question about David's son (12:35–37) specifically to scribal authorities because they are the experts in matters of Davidic messiahship (12:35). In support of his position he quotes Ps. 110:1: "The Lord [meaning God] said to my Lord [meaning Messiah], sit at my right hand" (12:36). Accordingly David, who is perceived as the author of the psalm, refers to the Messiah in terms of "my Lord." But if the Messiah is the Lord of David, how can he be the son of David (12:37)? He who will be "sitting at the right hand of Power" (14:62) cannot be the son of David. The Davidic issue is resolved. Jesus has not come to ordain the kingdom of David on Mount Zion in Jerusalem but to proclaim the Kingdom of God "to all the nations."

The refutation of the scribal doctrine of Davidic messiahship is immediately followed by the denunciation of the scribes (12:38–40). Their lifestyle and religious practices are now under attack. Those who espouse the Davidic identity of the Messiah lead lives in pursuit of personal power and prestige. Not unlike the disciples, who dream of honor and places of power, the scribal authorities regard religion as the art of self-advancement. Implacably egoistical, they exploit widows under the pretense of piety. The widow's offering (12:41–44) forms the ideal opposite to the scribal establishment and to the rich who give out of their abundance. Jesus calls the disciples' attention to her offering (12:43) because she gives "her whole living" (12:44). The disciples must know that it is the poor widow, and not the rich and the temple authorities, who exemplifies genuine discipleship.

In summing up Jesus' temple activity we observe that the Kingdom has been dissociated from the Jerusalem temple. We have seen Jesus make three trips to the temple. On his first trip he surveyed everything, then withdrew. On his second trip he judged and disqualified the temple. On his third trip he defined and defended his own authority above and against that of the

temple and its power structure. Far from leading to his enthronement in the temple as the Davidic Messiah, Jesus' temple activity
results in his separation from the temple. The Kingdom of God
and the temple are irreconcilably opposed to each other. Only
two persons, a male and a female, have endorsed Jesus' temple
teaching—the scribe who adopts Jesus' fundamental article of
faith and the widow who lives according to it. The acceptance of
male and female into the new community bids defiance to the old
all-male power structure of the chief priests, scribes, elders,
Herodians, Pharisees, and Sadducees.

PREDICTION OF TEMPLE DESTRUCTION

Having disqualified the temple and its custodians, having compared the temple to the dead fig tree, having made the point
that it was not the "right time" for the Kingdom in the temple,
having formulated the new article of faith, having detached his
identity from Davidic expectations, and having explicated his
own authority in opposition to the temple, Jesus now exits the
temple for the last time, never again to return to it (13:1). No
sooner has he made his exit than one of the disciples exults over
the might and glory of the temple complex: "Teacher, look, what
stones and what buildings!" (13:1). In view of the fact that
Jesus has just manifestly dissociated himself from the temple
and pronounced judgment on it, this statement on the lips of one
disciple must be considered a case of misplaced admiration, in
fact of gross misunderstanding. The disciple has eyes only for
the temple stones, and not for Jesus, the cornerstone of the new
temple.

Jesus' response is not long in coming: "Do you see these mighty
buildings? There will not be left here one stone upon another
that will not be pulled down" (13:2). This prediction of the physical destruction of the temple marks the logical culmination of
Jesus' entire temple activity. Now it should be clear to the disciple what has long been obvious to the reader: the temple, like the
fig tree, will be brought to ruin. As the tree has withered "from
the roots up," so will the temple be left not "one stone upon

another." Having made the fatal prediction, Jesus takes his place
on the Mount of Olives (13:3), the site from which he undertook
his journeys into the temple. Alarmed over Jesus' forecast, Peter,
James, John, and Andrew, the very disciples who were first
called to follow Jesus (1:16–20), now ask a crucial question:
"Tell us, when will these things be, and what will be the sign
when all these things are to be accomplished?" (13:4). "These
things" in the first part of the question refers back to the predicted destruction of the temple, while the accomplishment of
"all these things" in the second part indicates the time of fulfillment, the arrival of the Kingdom. Rendered into nontechnical
language the disciples' question asks, "Tell us, when will the
downfall of the temple be, and what will be the sign of the coming of the Kingdom?" It is in answer to this question that Jesus
delivers a lengthy speech while sitting on the Mount of Olives
(13:5–37).

The nature of the disciples' question and the corresponding
speech require a special word of explanation. The reader who
has followed the Markan story up to this point will notice that
part of Jesus' speech seems out of character with the Gospel's
biographical narration. Wars and rumors of war, uprisings and
revolts, earthquakes and famines, the establishment of a desolating sacrilege, flight into the mountains, and the appearance of
false prophets—these and other experiences are not what Mark
normally associates with the life of Jesus. What surfaces in
Jesus' speech, especially in its first part (13:5–23), is less the
story of Jesus and more that of early Christians. The reason
Jesus' biography ruptures, and ruptures at this moment, is that it
has reached a point where it touches on problems in Mark's
lifetime and that of his readers. The issue raised by the four
disciples projects us into the time of Mark and reveals a particular anxiety some forty years after the life and death of Jesus.
The disciples' question concerning the end of the temple and
the accomplishment of all things assumes a connection between
the destruction of the temple and the arrival of the Kingdom.
This assumption is not as strange as it may seem, if one reads it
in the context of first-century Jewish history. Josephus, the

Jewish historian who wrote most extensively on the Roman-Jewish War (A.D. 66–74), reports that Jewish defense strategies were motivated by religious considerations as much as by military ones. What gave many people the hope to fight against all odds was a deep-seated conviction of the imminent coming of the Messiah. Prophetic personalities promised messianic intervention throughout the war and messianic deliverance at the peak of the final battle over the temple of Jerusalem. This experience forms the background to the disciples' question concerning a connection between the crisis of the temple and the coming of the Messiah. If, as Jesus has predicted, the temple will be destroyed, will that catastrophe signal the coming of the Kingdom?

The speech proper opens with a warning against certain persons who appear in the name of Jesus saying, "I am he!" (13:5–6). They are people who claim messianic power and announce the presence of the Kingdom. A similar situation is reflected in 13:21–22. Prophetic personalities make an appearance saying, "Look, here is the Christ!" and "Look, there he is!" The experienced reader will recognize in 13:5–6 and 13:21–22 yet another instance of Markan framing composition. Both passages relate to one and the same kind of messianic prophets. By enclosing the first part of Jesus' speech (13:5–23) with references to these prophets, Mark suggests a connection between their activities and the events described in 13:7–20.

What appears to be reflected in 13:7-20 is the Roman-Jewish War (13:7–13), the destruction of the temple (13:14), and an ensuing period of great "tribulation" (13:15–20). Wars, rumors of wars, famines, persecutions, and the breakdown of families are all events reminiscent of the disastrous years of the Roman-Jewish War. Verse 13:14, couched in mysteriously guarded language, alludes to an extraordinary incident: "But when you see the 'desolating sacrilege' standing where he must not—let the reader understand—then those who are in Judea must flee to the mountains." The "desolating sacrilege," conceived as a personal power and standing where forbidden, will be a coded reference to the Roman general Titus who commanded the final assault on the temple and took possession of the ruined site (A.D. 70). The

phrase "let the reader understand" (Mark's only direct appeal
to the reader!) further underscores the unique nature of what is
intimated in 13:14. If, as we suggest, the Gospel was indeed
written in the aftermath of the temple destruction, then the
reader will undoubtedly catch the meaning of Jesus' mysterious
prediction. In other words Mark makes this and only this piece
of information speak most directly to his readers because it
portends what is uppermost in their minds. The destruction of the
temple will not be the end, but the beginning of a period of unprecedented crisis, the time of the great "tribulation" (13:15–20).

Mark's framing arrangement, we remember, suggests a connection between the messianic prophets and the turmoil of the
Roman-Jewish War. By bracketing the history of the war with
references to the messianic prophets, Mark develops the kind of
situation which we have already deduced from the disciples'
question (13:4). The prophets were active during the war years,
feeding the war efforts with messianic ideology. But the reader
will observe that the Markan Jesus denounces the prophets,
calling them "false prophets" (13:21) and convicting them of
deception. He reinforces his disagreement further by punctuating
his review of the Roman-Jewish War with such warning clauses
as "but the end is not yet" (13:7), "this is but the beginning of
the birth-pangs" (13:8), and "the gospel must first be preached
to all the nations" (13:10). The primary function of the first part
of the speech is to refute the prophets and to dissociate all Kingdom expectations from the war years. The war will bring suffering and death, not the full time of the Kingdom. In direct answer to the disciples' question (13:4) Jesus anticipates the temple
disaster as a nonmiraculous event (13:14). It will usher in a time
of flight, hardship, and tribulation, but not the Kingdom of God.

But prospects for the coming of the Kingdom are not altogether
discouraged. After he has disentangled false messianic hopes
from the war and the demise of the temple, the Markan Jesus
offers new hope for the future. "In those days, after that tribulation" (13:24), Jesus the Son of man will make his appearance in
power and in glory, and establish his Kingdom for all the nations
(13:24–27). Only then—after defeat, destruction, and tribula-

tion—can the fig tree once again serve as a symbol of hope (13:28–29). The coming of the Kingdom, although expected to be near, is nevertheless not subject to human calculation. Watchful responsibility is the code word for those who live in the days of the absence of "the master of the house" (13:30–37).

SUMMARY

In Mark 11:1—13:37 we have observed Jesus' arrival in Jerusalem and his exceptional dealings with the temple. The entire activity of his three temple journeys has been designed to drive a wedge between the temple, fallen prey to human corruption, and the Kingdom of God, pitted against the temple. The Kingdom of God is not to be associated with the temple or its authorities, neither in Jesus' time nor any time thereafter. The reader is advised not to read the Markan polemic against the temple in terms of an anti-Jewish bias. We must remember that the Markan Jesus had endorsed the ideal community consisting of Jews and Gentiles alike. His anger is directly focused at the temple authorities, most certainly not at his fellow Jews. Furthermore we observed that Mark's negative attitude toward the temple will have been motivated by the experience of the Roman-Jewish War (A.D. 66–74) and the Roman annihilation of the temple (A.D. 70). While during and toward the end of the war the temple increasingly served as the focal point of messianic hopes of liberation, these hopes went up in flames in the disaster of A.D. 70. That is the historical experience in the background of Mark's Gospel. By having Jesus predict the war, the temple destruction, and the nonarrival of the Kingdom in Jerusalem, Mark enables his readers, living after A.D. 70, to come to terms with the crisis in the context of the story of Jesus. Jesus' mission in Jerusalem was primarily designed to make the point that the temple was not to be the site of the Kingdom of God, neither in Jesus' own time nor in Mark's time. Jerusalem, far from being the place of the Kingdom, was to become the site of a double trauma, the death of Jesus and the death of the temple.

5
The Coronation
in
Humiliation

MARK 14:1—16:8

The so-called passion narrative, 14:1—16:8, brings the conflict between Jesus and the disciples to a head. Jesus loses his life and thereby saves it, while the disciples try to save their lives but lose. They fail to reach the goal of the journey, Galilee. Mark's story ends with the triumph of Jesus and the downfall of the disciples.

PREPARATIONS FOR DEATH

— ✓

Mark's passion narrative is shrouded in darkness, gloom, and tragedy. More than in Matthew, Luke, and John, his is the story of an execution, of the victim's Godforsakenness, and of the demise of the victim's closest followers. There is an oppressive air hovering over the final days, and almost no relief from the horror of death. Divine intervention is not forthcoming during Jesus' hours of suffering. The heavenly voice which sounded at baptism (1:11) and on the mount of transfiguration (9:7) is silent during the agony on the cross. There is, as we shall see, no resurrection appearance to lighten up and overcome the anguish. Death has cast its long shadow almost to the very end of the

Markan story. Jesus' resurrection is announced (16:6) but the resurrected Lord neither appears nor speaks to the disciples. Instead of a triumphal resurrection scene the gospel story concludes with an aborted message which seals the fate of the disciples (16:7-8).

With the opening verses (14:1-2) Mark leaves little doubt in the reader's mind that Jesus' journey is unto death. After the announced death plot in Galilee (3:6) and the authorities' violent reaction to Jesus' disqualification of the temple (11:18), this is now the third time that the opponents' intention to take his life is disclosed. What had long been anticipated by Jesus (2:20; 8:31; 9:31; 10:33) will come to pass in Jerusalem.

Jesus himself is located in Bethany (14:3) at the Mount of Olives (cf. 11:1), the place from which he had undertaken his three journeys into the temple. In Bethany a woman honors him by pouring oil over his head (14:3-9). Her anointment immediately brings to mind the ancient ritual of royal enthronement. Anointment, the pouring of oil over the head, was the central act by which the kings of Israel were appointed and installed into the royal office. David was made king by Samuel's anointment (1 Sam. 16:13), and his successors were the "anointed ones" of God (Ps. 45:7; 89:20). In analogy to this ancient ritual, the royal Davidic Messiah was likewise expected to be appointed by the royal investiture of anointment. Jesus' anointment at Bethany dramatically reverses all aspects of the Davidic appointment ceremony. He is not anointed in the temple but at "his place," outside of and opposite to Jerusalem and its temple. His is not a celebration in royal glitter and priestly pomp but a table fellowship in the house of a leper. He is anointed not by the priests or the high priest but by an anonymous woman. His anointment is not applauded but criticized. Above all, he is not anointed to power and life but "beforehand for the burial" (14:8). His is an anointment unto death. Just as the Kingdom of God was established in opposition to Jerusalem expectations and authorities, and as Jesus' authority was defined over against the temple, so his anointment at Bethany is in defiance of the traditional Davidic anointment. As indicated by his travels from the Mount of Olives

to the temple and back to the Mount of Olives, his purpose is not
to fulfill traditional Davidic expectations but to upset and reverse them. His installation into the royal office occurs at death,
not in life.

After Jesus' anointment, events are set into motion which will
precipitate his death, and thereby his coronation at death. Judas
Iscariot, known to the reader since his unfavorable introduction
(3:19), takes the initiative to deliver Jesus into the hands of
his opponents (14:10–11). Three times Judas features in connection with Jesus' death, and three times Mark shocks his readers
into the realization that it was one of the appointed leaders and
original insiders who cooperated with the priestly power structure. Judas was "one of the Twelve," "one of the Twelve," "one
of the Twelve" (14:10, 20, 43)!

In preparation for the last visit to Jerusalem prior to his death,
Jesus sends two disciples ahead with special instructions. The
disciples find everything as anticipated by Jesus, and they carry
out his directions (14:12–16). These rather intricate arrange-
ments parallel those made in advance of Jesus' first visit to Jerusalem. After arrival at the Mount of Olives, we remember, Jesus
had sent two disciples into the city to arrange for his entry, and
they had found everything as forecast by Jesus (11:1–6). The
first and the last time Jesus enters Jerusalem prior to death, he
makes careful preparations and takes special responsibilities.
These two visits are thereby singled out from among all other
visits to Jerusalem. The first visit, we recall, had set the stage for
Jesus' subsequent dealings with the temple, culminating in his
prediction of the destruction of the temple. The last visit sets the
stage for his own impending death, solemnly intoned during
the last meal. Jesus' first and last visits therefore epitomize the
double motive for his journey to Jerusalem: to announce the
death of the temple and to suffer death himself.

The immediate purpose for Jesus' trip to Jerusalem is to celebrate a last meal with the Twelve (14:17–25). The two disciples
had intended a Passover (14:12) and Jesus had agreed (14:14).
What in fact Jesus celebrates, however, is definitely not a cus-
tomary Passover and hardly what the disciples had expected.

This last meal is as little a traditional Passover as the Kingdom
of God is like the kingdom of father David, or the anointment at
Bethany was like the expected royal investiture. Whatever they
are eating, their meal is not centered around the paschal lamb,
and Jesus' words do not commemorate the Exodus events. Instead Jesus drastically recasts .the traditional Passover in view
of his death.

First Jesus discloses the presence of the traitor among the
Twelve (14:17–21). While the reader knows his identity the
eleven among the Twelve do not, because the Markan Jesus
refrains from revealing it to them. By withholding his identification from the disciples, Mark heightens the suspense and deepens
the tragedy of the Twelve. Instead of celebrating a joyous Passover they all find themselves under suspicion, one after the other
wondering, "Is it I?" (14:19). Not one of the Twelve is above
suspicion. Next Jesus defines and distributes bread and cup, the
symbols of his death (14:22–25). By eating the bread and drinking the cup, the Twelve are not only informed of Jesus' death
but all are made to share in it. And yet the statement "they all
drank from it" (14:23) is not without irony, because their conduct
during Jesus' passion belies their sharing of the cup. "They *all*
drank from it," but "they *all* forsook him" (14:50).

For the last time Jesus and the Twelve return to the Mount of
Olives (14:26). Speaking at "his place," and speaking for the last
time to the Twelve, Jesus announces the final events and the
goal of the journey (14:26–28). He will be killed and the disciples
will flee, but his resurrection will signal their return to Galilee.
The disclosure of the goal of Galilee accords an encompassing
logic to Jesus' mission and gives meaning to his whole journey.
Galilee had been the place of the founding of the ecumenical
Jewish-Gentile community. It had been in Galilee that the disciples were appointed apostolic shepherds over this new community. All along the way Jesus had prepared the disciples, and
especially the Twelve, for the time when they ought to assume
responsibility for a people who were "like sheep without a shepherd" (6:34). After the death of the shepherd he, Jesus, would
show them the way back to Galilee, and what had only been "the

beginning of the gospel" (1:1) of the Kingdom would then be completed.

Jesus' last words to the Twelve are not fully accepted by the Twelve. With spare but carefully measured language Mark sketches the subsequent confrontation between Peter and Jesus (14:29–31). Not unlike the earlier confrontation at Caesarea Philippi (8:27–33) Peter and Jesus refute each other, but this time all other eleven agree with Peter against Jesus. Peter, the spokesman of the Twelve, protests Jesus' prediction of the disciples' flight. He, Peter, would be superior over all others. Jesus rejects Peter's claim and predicts his imminently forthcoming denial. In turn Peter reverses Jesus' forecast. Far from denying Jesus, he would suffer and even die with him, "and they all said the same" (14:31).

Subtly but methodically Mark bears upon his readers, persuading them to accept the ultimate demise of the Twelve. Peter, the appointed leader, will deny Jesus, and the eleven are as mistaken about their future roles as they are deaf to Jesus' last instructions. At this stage one can no longer single out Judas as a scapegoat. He is but "one of the Twelve." The eleven have sided with Peter who contradicted Jesus' last instructions. It does not seem likely under these circumstances that the Twelve will be able to function as Jesus' apostolic representatives. There has been no improvement on their earlier state of blindness and deafness. Unless there is a last-minute change of heart, the Twelve will not reach the goal of the journey.

PARTING OF WAYS AT GETHSEMANE

Gethsemane at the Mount of Olives marks Jesus' last attempt to resolve the conflict between him and the disciples. But instead of the hoped-for reconciliation, Mark reports a final parting of the ways (14:32–42). Fear of his impending death drives Jesus into solitary prayer. Peter, James, and John, in the meantime, called to stay awake with Jesus, have fallen asleep. Three times Jesus moves from his place of prayer toward the Three, and each time he finds them asleep.

On his first return to the three disciples Jesus singles out Peter and criticizes him for his inability to stay awake (14:37). Significantly, this last time Jesus speaks to Peter, in the wake of their disagreement (14:29–31) and after finding him asleep, Jesus reverts to Peter's old name. Jesus' reproach is addressed to Simon, not to Peter. As the bestowal of the new name at the appointment of the Twelve had signaled Peter's ascendancy to leadership position, so the one and only recurrence of the old name signifies his demotion.

Jesus' second return to the Three highlights again their sleeping condition. The depth of their sleep is emphatically expressed: "for their eyes were very heavy" (14:40). Moreover Mark states that the Three "did not know what to answer him" (14:40). This reaction is reminiscent of Peter's incomprehension in view of Jesus' transfiguration (9:6). The Three understand what transpires at Gethsemane as little as they had earlier comprehended the significance of Jesus' transfiguration. They do not know how to respond properly to Jesus at Gethsemane, not merely out of natural drowsiness but due to their failure to grasp the meaning of the occasion. At the outset of Jesus' third return attention is drawn one more time to the weariness of the Three: "Are you still sleeping and taking your rest?" (14:41).

What is at stake in Gethsemane is the very issue which had proven a major stumbling block to discipleship: the necessity of suffering. For the last time Jesus attempts to unite his fate and that of the disciples into one common purpose. But whereas Jesus prayerfully resolves to drink the cup, the Twelve evade it. Relentlessly Mark accentuates the weakness of the three leaders. His chief purpose in dramatizing Jesus' three visits is to reinforce the negative roles played by the Three. Jesus' thrice-told visits demonstrate the recurrent and incorrigible blindness of the Three. Three times they oversleep the very hour in which Jesus comes to terms with his identity as suffering Son of man. If they fail to wake during this crucial hour of Jesus' passion prayer, how will they tolerate the hour of his passion? Gethsemane provides a telling refutation of the disciples' earlier pledge that they would all die with Jesus (14:31). In the end Jesus remains determined to walk the way to death, while the Three remain incapable of endorsing this way. The conflict between Jesus and the disciples has been brought to a head and proven insoluble. Henceforth Jesus and the disciples will go different ways. Jesus will be arrested and led into the city to his death. He will die and through death enter into life. The disciples will abandon Jesus at the occasion of his arrest and thus forfeit their last chance for entering upon the way to the Kingdom.

DEATH IN GODFORSAKENNESS

Jesus' passion proper begins with his arrest (14:43–50). Judas, leader of an armed crowd dispatched by the temple authorities, arrives at Gethsemane and identifies Jesus with a kiss. Jesus protests the atmosphere of violence and rejects all political implications. He is a teacher of authority, not a political insurrectionist (14:48; cf. 11:17; 12:13–17). His disciples not unexpectedly "all forsook him and fled" (14:50) the very moment the opponents lay hands on him. They had *all* drunk of the cup (14:23), they had *all* pledged to die with him (14:31), yet they *all* abandon him at the outset of his passion (14:50). Not following Jesus, they cannot reach the goal of the way. Their flight marks the end of their way of discipleship.

There are, however, two persons who do attempt to follow. One is the mysterious young man (14:51–52). While following Jesus he is apprehended by the authorities, but manages a narrow escape. In the midst of arrest, flight, and disintegration, he intimates rescue from death and ultimate reintegration. He escapes naked by leaving his linen cloth behind. In similar fashion Jesus is wrapped in a linen cloth (15:46) from which he escapes by resurrection. The young man will reappear at the end of the gospel story, sitting in the tomb and announcing Jesus' resurrection (16:5–7). The other person following Jesus is Peter. He is the only disciple who follows Jesus on his last journey into Jerusalem. Yet Peter follows "at a distance" (14:54) and then denies Jesus.

Upon arriving in Jerusalem Jesus is placed before the council, which is made up of representative temple authorities and pre-

sided over by the high priest (14:53–65). Their explicit intention
is to press for the death sentence. Inevitably Jesus' previous dealings with and in the temple become a major issue in the hearing
(14:57–59). The charge is that he would destroy the temple and
build another one in three days (14:58). On the face of it this
statement appears to conform to the facts of Jesus' life. Had he
not disqualified the temple and announced his resurrection after
three days? To be sure, he had denounced the temple and predicted its physical downfall. But the witnesses confuse the Jesus
who condemned the temple with a Jesus who is supposed to be
the personal agent of the temple destruction. He had never said
that he would personally bring about the fall of the temple. Moreover he had predicted his resurrection three days after his death,
and not a temple three days after the fall of the old one. Hence
the witnesses do not speak the truth (14:56, 59), and Jesus remains silent in the face of their falsehood. ,

At this point the high priest personally takes command of the
hearing and steers it toward confession and death sentence. He
elicits Jesus' confession by asking the crucial messianic question: "Are you the Christ, the Son of the Blessed?" that is, the
Son of God (14:61). Jesus answers with an emphatic "I am,"
but in the same breath adds a qualification: "You will see the
Son of man seated at the right hand of Power, and coming with
the clouds of heaven" (14:62). This confession deeply upsets the
high priest and offends his religious convictions. Jesus' reply in
terms of "I am" and "you will see" both confirms his present
authority and anticipates his future revelation. He is the Christ,
the Son of God, standing at death's door, but under the circumstances he is not recognizable to the council members. The
time will come, however, when his status will be universally
manifest. As for this future, Jesus speaks mysteriously of himself as the Son of man in the third person. As Son of man he will
be exalted to the right hand of God, and he will come in heavenly
power and glory. This kind of Messiah hardly agrees with the
high priest's conception of messiahship. Jesus' virtual identification with God appears as blasphemous as his earlier claim to
forgive sins (2:7). In sorrowful anger the high priest tears his robe

and without difficulty obtains a unanimous vote in favor of Jesus'
death (14:64).

All along the way Jesus had revealed his identity and the purpose of his journey to the disciples, the Twelve, and the Three.
But the insiders had turned out to be outsiders, and Peter, the
leader, a false confessor. As for the crowds and his opponents,
Jesus had never disclosed his identity to either of them. Only the
evil spirits had recognized him, but Jesus had ordered them to
keep silent (1:34; 3:11–12). In the perspective of the total gospel
story, Jesus' confession before the high priest climaxes a life
haunted by misunderstanding, false confessions, mistaken identity, and false accusations. The one and only time Jesus confesses
his full identity before his opponents at the hearing, he promptly
incriminates himself and draws the death sentence. That is of
course the way it must be, according to Mark's conception of
Jesus' messiahship. The one and only self-revelation before his
accusers must be "certified" with the death sentence, because
it is in the light of and as a result of his death that Jesus ac-
complishes his identity as Son of God and Son of man.

Abandoned by his followers and confronted with false accusers,
Jesus is condemned to death at the same time that Peter denies
him, and in the very same place. Mark enacts this understanding
with his favorite framing technique which we have observed before. He enclosed the story of Jesus' hearing (14:55–65) with two
parts of the story of Peter's denials (14:54, 66–72). By means of
this framing arrangement Mark juxtaposed Jesus' confession and
Peter's rejection, and invited the reader to compare the two
scenes. The net effect is an incomparable dramatization of the
depth of Peter's tragedy. This last time the leader of the Twelve
features in the gospel story, he is placed in irreconcilable opposition to Jesus. Peter's anticonfessions are pitted against Jesus'
fateful confession. Jesus' confession incurs the death sentence,
whereas Peter's three denials are attempts to save his life.

Three times, we recall, Jesus had attempted to open the eyes of
the disciples, and especially of the Twelve, to the reality of his
impending suffering (8:31; 9:31; 10:33–34). Three times they
had remained imperceptive. Three times at Gethsemane Jesus

had asked the Three to stay awake during his hour of passion prayer (14:32–42). But each time Jesus had found them overcome by sleep. Peter's three denials mark the very peak of the discipleship tragedy. After a history of persistent and incurable blindness the disciples abandon Jesus, one betrays him, and Peter, the leader of the Twelve, in his last appearance denies Jesus three times while Jesus confesses. Brokenhearted and weeping, Peter is phased out of the gospel story. He knows he has fulfilled Jesus' dire prediction (14:30, 72).

At the instigation of the temple authorities and the council members Jesus is bound and delivered to Pontius Pilate (15:1). The Roman governor is in charge of the occupation troops and sensitive to the issue of civil law and order. If he can be convinced of the political nature of Jesus' crime, the latter is punishable by the Roman death penalty of crucifixion. Pilate asks what from his viewpoint is a political question: "Are you the King of the Jews?" (15:2). Had Jesus assumed royal, political powers and thereby posed a threat to Roman law and order? Jesus' reply appears ambiguous (15:2). While he is King, he is not the kind of king Pilate envisages. The governor "wonders" about Jesus (15:5) and offers his release in the place of Barabbas, a man of violence (15:6–10); indeed Pilate still "wonders" even after Jesus has died (15:44). But the temple authorities, who with the help of Judas had masterminded the arrest and conviction, stir up the crowds against Jesus (15:11–15). Pilate yields to pressure and issues the penalty reserved for political criminals. Falsely confessed and falsely accused all his life, Jesus dies a victim of mistaken identity.

While the evangelist does not dwell on the physical aspect of Jesus' death, the agony he describes is of a force which exceeds that of physical suffering. Jesus dies abandoned by all and assisted by none. Simon of Cyrene, who carries the cross, does not act out of pity but has to be coerced into this service (15:21). The soldiers, indifferent to Jesus' agony, divide his garments after they have done their job (15:24). Passersby taunt Jesus to perform a self-serving miracle (15:29–30). The temple authorities ridicule his nonmiraculous death (15:31–32). Not even the two outlaws crucified to the right and left can bring themselves to sympathize with Jesus (15:32). His final words are misinterpreted (15:34–35), and at the last a cruel attempt is made to prolong his life (15:36). Surrounded by a chorus of mockers, Jesus suffers and dies, rejecting the one drink which was meant to alleviate his torments (15:23). He came "not to be served but to serve, and to give his life as a ransom for many" (10:45).

From the sixth to the ninth hour darkness envelops the cross and covers the whole land (15:33). This global darkness illustrates the triumph of the forces of evil and the demonic seizure of power. At the cross demonic forces rule in supremacy, and Jesus is crushed by the very powers which he himself had come to exorcise. His last two cries, the cry of dereliction (15:34) and the cry of expiration (15:37), also depict him as being overpowered by the forces of evil. Both are "loud cries" which are uttered in a state of surrender to the evil spirits (cf. 1:26; 5:7). As Jesus' authority formerly caused demons to convulse, so does the demonic presence at the cross make him cry out into utter darkness.

Engulfed in demonic darkness and overcome by the forces of evil, Jesus suffers the absence of God: "My God, my God, why hast thou forsaken me?" (15:34). His last articulate words are in the form of a question put to God, who had given him power at baptism and left him powerless at the cross. He is "delivered up" (14:10, 11, 18, 21, 41, 42, 44; 15:1, 10, 15) not merely into the hands of the Roman-Jewish power structure but beyond that into demonic darkness and Godforsakenness. He suffers not merely physical pain and desertion by friends and followers but beyond that utter aloneness. God's nonintervention, his abandonment of Jesus in the hour of greatest need, constitutes the ultimate depth of Jesus' suffering. With his last question left unanswered, Jesus utters the cry of dereliction and dies.

THE CRUCIFIED KING

Rejected by his followers, taunted by his enemies, derided even by those who suffer the cross next to him, delivered into the hands of Satan, and abandoned by God, Jesus paradoxically fulfills his royal mission. Perhaps the most conspicuous device employed by

Mark to convey this paradox is the opponents' use of the term
king in addressing Jesus. While mistaking his identity they
thereby unwittingly confirm the truth about him. Pilate, the
man who ratifies the death sentence, is the first person to refer
to Jesus as king (15:2). The crowd which demands the crucifixion
is reported to have called him king (15:12). The soldiers enact a
cruel mock scene in which they salute Jesus as king (15:16–20).
The temple authorities, principal promoters of his death, ridicule
him as king (15:31–32). In short the very people who are instru-
mental in Jesus' death—the temple authorities, Pilate, the soldiers,
and the crowd—confer the royal designation upon him and thereby
speak and enact the truth in ignorance and infamy. For Mark,
Jesus is precisely the man who suffers coronation through humiliation and whose crown is made of thorns. The Kingdom he had
proclaimed in Galilee (1:14–15) and for which he had—without
success—prepared the Twelve is legitimized by his death on the
cross. Far from contradicting his message of the Kingdom, Jesus'
crucifixion is paradoxically the moment of his coronation.

There are additional features which strengthen Mark's interpretation of the cross as place of enthronement. Jesus' journey to
Jerusalem is conceived as a "going up" (10:32, 33; 15:41) toward
suffering and cross. Hanging on the cross he refuses to comply
with the taunters' appeal to "come down" (15:30, 32) from the
cross. This going up–coming down scheme designates the cross
as his chosen place of elevation. Moreover the crucifixion of the
two outlaws, "one on his right and one on his left" (15:27), en-
hances the image of an enthronement scene. Likewise the inscription centrally placed over the cross (15:26) states the crime but
ironically reveals his honor. His messiahship is consummated in
total abandonment on the cross.

Jesus' death has two immediate consequences. It coincides
with the rending of the temple curtain (15:38) and effects the
centurion's confession (15:39). As for the rending of the curtain,
Markan language indicates that it is not the one covering the
innermost sanctuary, the holy of holies, but rather the one hanging in front of the whole temple building. The tearing "in two,
from top to bottom" (15:38) of the curtain illustrates the ruin of
the temple as a whole. We recall that the Markan Jesus had had

a double motive for his coming to Jerusalem. He came to announce the death of the temple and to suffer death himself. His death on the cross brings these two motives into a causal relationship and thereby resolves the objective of his journey to Jerusalem. By dying a death instigated by the temple authorities, he precipitates the demise of the authorities' traditional place of power. His own death in powerlessness anticipates the destruction of the temple and establishes him as King above and against it. As for the centurion's words of exclamation, they form the only true confession made by a human being in the Gospel. The nature of Jesus and the purpose of his journey is revealed in view of his death. According to Mark the essence of Jesus can only be revealed in view of his death. For this reason the disciples never came to recognize Jesus, the crucified King, Son of God. They had abandoned him at the outset of his last and crucial journey into Jerusalem. And so it is once again left to the enemy—paradoxically, to the man in charge of the execution—to make the confession the disciples should have made but could not make. Seeing the manner of Jesus' dying and the circumstances surrounding his death, the centurion confesses that "the man was Son of God."

Whereas the disciples of John the Baptist had buried their master in a tomb (6:29), Jesus' disciples do not pay him this last reverence. It is once again a representative of the forces of destruction who does what the disciples should have done. Joseph of Arimathea, "a respected member of the council" (15:43), arranges Jesus' burial with the cooperation of Pilate and the centurion. Since Mark and only Mark among the evangelists states that *all* the council members had approved the death sentence (14:64), he at least implies that Joseph, this respected council member, also cast his vote against Jesus. But under the impact of Jesus' death Joseph of Arimathea, "himself looking for the Kingdom" (15:43), obtains the body and assures its burial in a tomb. One last time an extreme outsider is drawn onto the way of the Kingdom, while the insiders fail.

In the absence of the Twelve, a group of Galilean women see the crucifixion "from afar" (15:40), observe the place of burial (15:47), and arrive at the tomb to anoint Jesus' body (16:1). One might well assume that these Galilean women will finally reverse the disciples' disintegration and thus bring the discipleship plot to a happy ending. Yet all indications point in the opposite direction. Instead of reorienting the disciples to the way of Jesus, the women reinforce and finalize their way toward destruction.

The women approach the tomb for the purpose of anointing Jesus' body. In Mark's story, however, Jesus has already been anointed "at his place" in Bethany by the hands of a woman. Mark had explicitly defined her act of pouring oil over Jesus' head as an anointment "beforehand for the burial" (14:8). Hence what the Galilean women had come to do has already been done by the anonymous woman beforehand. Indeed if Jesus was to become King on the cross, and not by burial or resurrection, he had to be anointed beforehand. By the time the women arrive at the tomb, Jesus has not only been anointed but also enthroned King on the cross and has overcome death by resurrection. While the women look for the dead body, Jesus has ceased to be a dead body; while they expect to find it in the tomb, he is no longer in the tomb. In part that is the message given to them by the young man sitting in the tomb: "He has risen, he is not here" (16:6).

The young man not only discredits the finality of the tomb but reorients the women toward the true goal of the journey: "Go, tell his disciples and Peter that he is going before you to Galilee; there you will see him, as he told you" (16:7). The last clause refers back to Jesus' last instruction given to the Twelve at the Mount of Olives (14:28). As predicted, Jesus had been resurrected and was now issuing the call to go back to Galilee. There, no doubt, the disciples should assume responsibility over the Jewish-Gentile community of the Kingdom of God. The message therefore which the women have to convey to the disciples and to Peter is that Jesus was resurrected and on the way to Galilee. But it is that message which the women fail to deliver. The one message designed to rescue the disciples founders on the failure of the women. As a consequence the disciples never learn that the signal had been given for the return to Galilee. The women's failure compounds that of the disciples and seals their own fate as well as that of the disciples. Overcome by trembling, astonishment, and fear, the women flee (16:8), as earlier all the disciples had fled (14:50).

Since ancient times heroic efforts have been made to avoid the inevitable conclusions that ought to be drawn from this ending of Mark's gospel. The feeling that the gospel could not have ended with 16:8 arose as early as the second century, when the so-called longer ending, 16:9–20, was added on to 16:1–8. This longer ending, dealing with Jesus' resurrection appearances, his reunion with the eleven, and his ascension into heaven, provided the final outcome that was felt to be missing in 16:1–8. After it was recognized that 16:9–20 was a secondary addition, scholars expended much time and energy in search for what was called the "lost ending," a text that was alleged to have brought to a happy resolution the unhappy events reported in 16:1–8. But scholars not only failed to discover the "lost ending," they also could not explain how this assumed original ending could ever have been lost. One very popular attempt to disprove the Markan ending at 16:8, finally, was to argue that grammatically a piece of literature cannot end in the manner Mark 16:8 does (with the particle *gar*). And yet we have found evidence in classical literature to the effect that a text can indeed end the way Mark 16:8 does. In view of the facts that 16:9–20 was not part of the original gospel and no authentic conclusion other than 16:1–8 was found, and strengthened also by cases of similar grammatical endings in ancient literature, scholarship has widely but not unanimously come to accept 16:1–8 as the original ending of Mark's gospel. There exists substantial manuscript evidence to support this thesis. Almost as important as the manuscript evidence, however, is the narrative logic of Mark's story. Does the story of an abortive message provide the fitting conclusion to Mark's dramatization of the conflict between Jesus and the disciples? Is it conceivable that Mark ends his story with the downfall of the disciples and not with their rehabilitation? In conclusion we shall recall the high points of Mark's discipleship plot and demonstrate the logical necessity of the ending at 16:8.

SUMMARY

On a Galilean mountain Jesus appoints twelve disciples to become his representatives. To a large extent Jesus uses his jour-

ney to teach these Twelve, and the Three among them and Peter,
everything they have to know in order to be able to function as
apostolic shepherds of the new community. Taking to heart what
Jesus says and following him on his way, the disciples will find
the key to the Kingdom of God. At the lakeside Jesus conveys
privileged information to the Twelve and a group of select insiders concerning the nature of the Kingdom. The mystery of the
Kingdom is that it is in the process of growth, fraught with disappointment and failure, yet nevertheless advancing toward full
maturity. The disciples, as active participants in the mystery of
the Kingdom, must know that they cannot expect it to be an
accomplished fact or to come immediately in power and in
glory. In a series of boat trips Jesus opens up the frontiers toward
the Gentiles and defines the communal identity of the Kingdom
of God. Jews and Gentiles, males and females shall live together
purged of evil and in unity. But the logic of these voyages finds
no congenial response among the disciples. As a consequence
Jesus charges them with hardness of heart, blindness of eyes,
and deafness of ears. Already at that point the reader is alerted
to the fact that the disciples may be incapable of representing
Jesus in the ongoing work of the Kingdom. If they do not grasp
the nature of the Kingdom, how can they assume responsibility
for it? Unless they have a change of heart and overcome their
blindness and deafness, theirs cannot be a happy ending.

On the way to Jerusalem Jesus discloses to the disciples, and
especially to the Twelve, what to expect in the city: he would
suffer, be delivered into the hands of the enemy, and be killed,
but he was also to rise from death. Furthermore he defines discipleship unambiguously in terms of following the suffering Jesus.
The disciples, under the leadership of Peter, consistently fail to
accept the suffering Jesus and the concept of suffering discipleship. Peter endorses a triumphalist Christ, and the disciples are
preoccupied with personal power and prestige. Manifestly, what
they expect in Jerusalem is the Kingdom as an accomplished
fact, in power and in glory. Yet if they do not follow Jesus all the
way, how can they hope to reach the goal?

Once in Jerusalem, Jesus and the disciples each play out their respective roles to their logical conclusions. Jesus makes it abundantly clear that Jerusalem and its temple is not to be the place of the Kingdom, and not the end of the journey. After Jesus' antitemple demonstration, how can the disciples continue investing hopes in Jerusalem and its temple? In his last instructions to the Twelve Jesus proclaims Galilee as the final destination. Then he suffers death on the cross and is enthroned King through death. With death behind him and his kingship assured, he signals the way to Galilee, the new community of the Kingdom of God. The disciples on the other hand act in accordance with their vision of the Kingdom in power. Far from experiencing a change of heart they betray, contradict, deny, and in the end abandon the suffering and dying Jesus. But having abandoned Jesus on the threshold of his passion, they miss the most important event of his journey into the Kingdom: his enthronement on the cross. The centurion, not the disciples, witnesses and confesses Jesus as Son of God. Unable to grasp the nature of the Kingdom and unable to come to terms with the concept and person of the crucified King, they have now missed his royal enthronement. There is no way that the disciples can become the leaders of the Kingdom of God.

After the disappearance of the disciples the women, acting in the place of the disciples, bring the disciples' tragedy to its logical conclusion. They fail to convey to the disciples the message of Jesus' resurrection and his return to Galilee. As a result of their failure the disciples never do return to Galilee. The Kingdom community in Galilee will not be represented by the disciples. Not going to Galilee they will do what they always had wanted to do, that is, stay in Jerusalem and wait there for the Kingdom to come in power. But this was against the express wishes of Jesus. Jerusalem was to be destroyed and the temple burnt to the ground. "For whoever would save his life will lose it; and whoever loses his life for my sake and the gospel's will save it" (8:35).

Conclusion

We began this book by noting the religious motivation of the four evangelists and the religious nature of their gospel compositions. Each evangelist *reinterprets* the life and death of Jesus for his own time and people. The result is four different gospel stories. Of these four the Markan story may well be the most startling. The reader who has followed our advice and read Mark's story from beginning to end will be puzzled and will wonder why this evangelist interprets the sacred past of Jesus and his closest followers in this extraordinary fashion. Why is Mark preoccupied with the Jerusalem temple and its destruction? Why does he locate the community of the Kingdom of God in a northern, Galilean area and not, for example, in Jerusalem? How can one account for his hostility toward the family of Jesus? Why this almost blasphemous theology of Jesus' death in God-forsakenness, and the staggering paradox of enthronement by utter humiliation? Above all, why this relentless narrative drive to undermine the authority of the disciples, and especially of Peter and the Twelve? How can a Christian author write a story which disgraces the Twelve, the representatives of Jesus? What could possibly be the good news of a story which ends with the bad news concerning the Twelve? In short, why does Mark tell this kind of story, and what is its religious significance for his readers in the first century, but also for us in the twentieth century?

Since Mark's story is essentially that of the conflict and break between Jesus and the Twelve, our initial question should pertain to the Twelve. Apart from Mark's interpretation of and disaffection with them, what was their role in early Christian history and where were they located? The first reference to Peter and the

Twelve is found in 1 Cor. 15:5. By general consent 1 Cor. 15:3–5 is not a Pauline formulation but a pre-Pauline confessional formula adopted by Paul. This oldest witness to Peter and the Twelve therefore dates back to a time before Mark wrote his Gospel and even before Paul wrote his First Letter to the Corinthians (ca. A.D. 55). Unfortunately 1 Cor. 15:5 does not link up the resurrection appearances to Peter and the Twelve with a specific place, but Jerusalem seems the likely setting since the formula mentions Jesus' death, burial, and resurrection, all events pointing to Jerusalem. It is from Luke-Acts that we learn of the existence of the Twelve in Jerusalem after Jesus' death and resurrection. According to Luke it was the church of Jerusalem which was founded on the leadership of the Twelve (Acts 1:24–26; 6:2) under the primacy of Peter (Acts 2:14, 37; 3:12; 4:8; 5:29). If Peter and the Twelve were (or were considered) the founding figures of the Jerusalem church, does Mark in reporting Jesus' estrangement from the Twelve thereby dissociate himself and his readers from the Jerusalem church? An answer to this question will depend on additional evidence of references to Jerusalem in Mark's Gospel. If such is forthcoming, we must then examine whether the entire gospel story is plausible as a polemic against the Jerusalem position.

We know from Paul's letter to the Galatians that there existed in Jerusalem a triumvirate of Three, three disciples who were the "pillars" of the church (Gal. 2:9). To be sure, the triumvirate reported by Paul does not in all points match the inner circle of Three mentioned in Mark. While, curiously, Paul and Mark specify three identical names (Peter, James, and John), the James named in Galatians is Jesus' brother, whereas the James in Mark is the son of Zebedee. Whatever the reason for this discrepancy, Mark's concept of a leadership structure of Twelve, and the Three among them, under the primacy of Peter, corresponds to the leadership situation of the Jerusalem church. Thus the evangelist's criticism of the Twelve, and especially of the Three and above all of Peter, could well be directed against the Jerusalem church. Mark also appears to have the Jerusalem community in mind when he separates the family of Jesus from

the Kingdom of God. According to Luke it was the Jerusalem
church which held members of Jesus' family in high esteem
(Acts 1:14). The failure of the Galilean women reported at the
conclusion of the Gospel is likewise intelligible from the perspective of the Jerusalem situation. According to Luke Galilean
women were members of the Jerusalem church (Acts 1:14). Moreover their failure, as narrated by Mark, compounds that of the
Twelve and effects an ongoing Christian presence in Jerusalem.
By not delivering the message of a return to Galilee, they elected
Jerusalem as the place of the Kingdom's arrival. That, according
to Mark, they should not have done. In sum, Mark's combined
critique of the Twelve, the Three, Peter, Jesus' family, and the
Galilean women is directed against people who are identifiable
as representative figures of the Jerusalem church. The logic of
Mark's critique is also aimed at the very existence of the Jerusalem community. Jesus' closest followers failed to understand
the nature of the Galilean community, abandoned Jesus, missed
his coronation on the cross, and were thus stalled in Jerusalem,
never reaching the goal of Galilee.

Among other issues reflecting Mark's disagreement with the
Jerusalem church are the Gentile mission, the abolition of ritual
taboos, and the focus on the cross. The Jerusalem church was
predominantly Jewish and, as is obvious from Paul's dealing
with its leaders, had difficulty in coming to terms with the Gentile
mission. The disciples in Mark, we recall, do not grasp Jesus'
breakthrough toward the Gentiles and incur Jesus' condemnation
of "hardness of heart." The majority of the Jewish Christians in
Jerusalem will have been loyal observers of the Jewish Law. Mark
overrules the laws of ritual cleanliness and pleads for the concept
of inward purity. Again, the disciples have trouble understanding
this concept, and the Markan Jesus expresses his disappointment. Finally, it seems doubtful whether the Jerusalem Christians
made much of the cross of Jesus. Politically, it was dangerous to
propagate the death of one crucified as a criminal in the city of
his execution. Religiously, more distance is required, mentally,
temporally, and spatially, before one can reflect back upon an
event as horrendous as the crucifixion. Instead the focus in Jeru-

salem will have been on Jesus as a messianic figure of power, crucified but resurrected, and present in the community as the resurrected Lord or expected to come in the near future. Mark, we remember, sharply criticizes the disciples for failing to endorse the suffering Jesus. In the end they abandon Jesus on the cross, opting instead for what they think will be the Kingdom in power.

If it is granted that Mark narrates a story which raises critical questions about the existence and nature of the Jerusalem church, we are forced to ask: How dare he? Why would he reinterpret the life and death of Jesus against Jesus' chosen representatives? Why would this Jewish Christian author who is undoubtedly sympathetic to the Christian cause want to deprive Christians of their sacred center? The clue lies in Mark's preoccupation with the temple of Jerusalem and its predicted destruction. We have shown that the Markan Jesus journeys to Jerusalem for a twofold purpose: to predict the death of the temple and to predict and suffer his own death. From the perspective of the Markan readers one prediction will have come true as much as the other. In other words we assume that the Gospel was written after A.D. 70, following the destruction of Jerusalem and its temple, and in full knowledge of the demise of the Jerusalem church. That is the reason Mark can be unreservedly against Jerusalem, against its temple, and against the disciples' presence in the city. He can dare argue that the disciples should not have stayed in Jerusalem after Jesus' resurrection, because he knows that the sacred center of the Christian movement has fallen a victim to Roman force and violence.

If we accept a postwar dating of the Gospel, Mark's case against the Jerusalem church takes on a deeper dimension. Viewed in light of the destruction of Jerusalem the Gospel does not pronounce judgment on the mother church as much as it seeks an explanation for its extinction. Mark is not vengeful, holding a personal grudge against the Twelve, but rather a prophetic type of writer who searches for an answer to a terrible crisis. It is from this perspective also that the religious significance of Mark's Gospel will come into full view.

If we transport ourselves back into the situation as it may have

presented itself to Christians after A.D. 70, the full impact of
the Gospel message will be felt. Israel is occupied by Roman
troops, Jerusalem is destroyed, and the temple burnt to the
ground. All messianic expectations which kindled and sustained
Jewish war efforts have remained unfulfilled. The specific
Christian hope that Jesus the Messiah would come to the rescue
was also dashed. Those prophets who predicted messianic intervention and liberation turn out in retrospect to be false prophets.
After the crucifixion the nonmiraculous experience of the fall of
Jerusalem is the second trauma suffered by early Christians. The
present is bleak and lacking an explanation for death and destruction. Unnerved by the hopelessness of the present, Mark turns
to the past, that is, the sacred past of Jesus. The evangelist is
convinced that the Jesus who forty years ago walked across
Galilee and died in Jerusalem holds the key to the traumatic
experience of A.D. 70. Therein lies the religious motivation for
and therapeutic quality of the writing of the gospel. A therapist
treating an individual who has suffered a breakdown will make
this person relive the past in search of clues to the present crisis.
In similar fashion Mark, living at a critical juncture in history,
makes his readers relive the life and death of Jesus in search of
an explanation for the breakdown of their religious center.

Reading Mark's story in the aftermath of the destruction of
Jerusalem, one learns that forty-odd years ago Jesus had announced the arrival of the Kingdom in Galilee. He had appointed
twelve disciples to feed and serve the people, and he had prepared them for the time after his death and resurrection. In
Jerusalem, on the other hand, Jesus had left no doubt whatso-
ever that it was not the city of the Kingdom. His whole life cul-
minated in a sharp disagreement with the temple authorities,
the disqualification of the temple, and the prediction of its
destruction. His own death, resulting from his denunciation of
the temple and initiated by the temple authorities, in turn anticipates the death of the temple. At the moment of his death the
temple curtain is torn asunder. The reader, living in the aftermath of the two traumas, is thus made to discern the deep logic

which connects the life of Jesus with the temple of Jerusalem, and the death of Jesus with that of the temple.

While the story of Jesus demonstrates the connection between the two traumas, the story of the disciples accounts for the fate of the Jerusalem church. Mark's discipleship dramatization clearly engages readers who have acknowledged the authority of the Twelve. At the outset the Twelve are introduced as authority figures in nonpolemical fashion. In this way the story meets the readers on their own ground. Once contact is established with the readers, the story unfolds a persistent and intensifying misperception by the disciples all the way to the tragic crescendo in the passion events. On a miniature scale this development from a neutral to a negative portrayal of the disciples is acted out in Peter's so-called confession. Initially, we recall, the reader is inclined to accept Peter's confession at face value. But the subsequent confrontation between Jesus and Peter brings the reader face to face with Jesus' confession as suffering Son of man and his condemnation of Peter as Satan. By retracing the journey of Jesus and his disciples, the readers are thus gradually and methodically prepared for a final parting of the ways. In reading the gospel one hopes that eventually the disciples will repent and believe in the gospel of the Kingdom. Yet the further we read the story, the more Mark discourages our hopes. After the dismal failure of the disciples at Jesus' passion, all remaining hopes focus on the final outcome of the story. The ending at least should bring rehabilitation and reconciliation. But Mark, instead of reversing the disciples' course, brings it to its logical conclusion. He has reserved the ending of the gospel to deliver the mortal blow to the fate of the disciples. At that moment, having read Mark's story from beginning to end, it must dawn on the reader that the disciples missed the way into the Kingdom. Their ongoing presence in Jerusalem is thus explained as a result not of the will of Jesus but of their failure to perceive the will of Jesus all along the way.

In the titular verse (1:1) Mark had stated his intention to write what was only "the beginning of the gospel." Now that the readers have relived the story of Jesus, their way must no longer concur with that of the Twelve. They know more than the disciples ever did, because Mark has given them the opportunity to learn from Jesus and his conflict with Peter and the Twelve. The readers, living after A.D. 70, have learned to understand the fall of the temple in connection with Jesus' life and death, and the demise of the Jerusalem church as a consequence of the abortive discipleship. Having undergone the gospel therapy, that is, knowing the cause of the crisis, they can turn from passive readers of the gospel of the Kingdom to active participants in the Kingdom of God. The crisis of Jerusalem did not put an end to the Kingdom, and for those who have read and believe in the gospel, the way is open to the new community. That is the gospel news! The Kingdom of God, far from having perished in the fall of Jerusalem, is an ongoing reality. It was called into existence by Jesus some forty years ago in Galilee, it has remained untouched by the destruction of Jerusalem, and it is accessible to all who have taken Mark's gospel to heart. One reason the gospel ends in this "incomplete" fashion is because the failure of the women is indeed not the last word on the story of the Kingdom. While the disciples' fate is sealed, the readers in Mark's time, who understand the nature of the crisis, are invited to complete the journey of Jesus left incomplete by the disciples. In this sense reading the Gospel is but the beginning of the gospel's actualization in real life.

Those who actualize the gospel message know that the new fellowship in the Kingdom is not what the Twelve thought it was going to be. The open space of Galilee symbolizes a freer spirit than that represented by the walled city of Jerusalem. The Kingdom is open to "all the nations," Jews and Gentiles, as well as to both males and females. It is not hierarchical in structure but egalitarian in nature. Its fundamental article of faith, love of God and love of neighbor, overrules all laws and regulations. Most importantly, its central authority is Jesus, who was enthroned not by the power of resurrection but in the humiliation of the cross. This crucified King teaches the lesson of service and suffering on behalf of others, not the art of self-aggrandizement.

It was the principal error of the disciples that they could not accommodate their expectations to the suffering and dying Jesus. Chastened by the cataclysmic event of the fall of Jerusalem, Mark dispenses with the disciples' Christ of power and instead *need today* reactivates the memory of the death of Jesus. Indeed it is precisely after the defeat by the Romans and the annihilation of the center that the Jesus who dies in Godforsakenness becomes the authentic representative of the Kingdom of God. The people who expected the Messiah to come to their rescue have experienced the terror of Godforsakenness. To them a Jesus who himself died forsaken by God is the believable Redeemer. He is not a Jesus who speaks cheap words of comfort or who glorifies power while denying death. Rather he is the Jesus who journeyed from vitality to agony, from a life in power into a nonmiraculous death. And just as he was enthroned King at the moment of humiliation, so can his followers enter his kingship in the midst of their own death and destruction.

We have suggested that the Gospel of Mark may be the most startling of the four Gospels in the New Testament. Its most surprising feature is the elimination of all authority figures who mediate between Jesus and the reader of the Gospel. There are altogether three mediating authorities: the relatives of Jesus, the messianic prophets, and the disciples. Mark opposes all three of them. He relegates the family representatives to the outside, calls the charismatic representatives false prophets, and argues the failure of the official representatives. This exclusion of the mediating powers concurs with the evangelist's intention to return to the beginnings of Jesus. Mark's theological enterprise, the rejection of tradition and the return to the origin, has a very familiar ring to it. It is strikingly reminiscent of Reformation theology—its opposition to tradition and return to the fundamentals. In addition we find both in Mark and in Reformation theology a strong emphasis on the theology of the cross. This striking resemblance between Mark and the Reformers is not the result of our imposition of Reformation categories upon Mark. Rather it results from the fact that both Mark and the Reformers wrote at a time of considerable cultural and political crisis. Whenever one rejects or suffers the loss of mediating authorities, the urge is to return to the original authority, while the shock of the loss reawakens our sensibilities to the reality of death.

While it is of course true that we do not live in a state of permanent crisis, Mark has discovered a truth of universal validity. All Christian churches, as they grow up and age, run the risk of growing apart from Jesus and his original message. But forgetting about the origin may result in mindless adjustments to the values of the contemporary culture. The disciples, as Mark sees them, fail to listen to the voice of Jesus and promptly adopt a whole system of self-serving values. Unless we let ourselves be reminded of Jesus' self-giving life and death, our religious institutions can develop an exaggerated sense of importance, and we as individuals may practice Christian faith as the way of self-improvement. It remains the abiding significance of Mark that he invites us back onto Jesus' journey which refreshes our memory of what Christianity was meant to be.